Professional Airbrush Techniques
with Vince Goodeve

Vince Goodeve

Published by:
Wolfgang Publications Inc.
217 Second Street North
Stillwater, MN 55082
www.wolfpub.com

D0898291

Legals

First published in 2006 by Wolfgang Publications Inc.,
217 Second Street North, Stillwater MN 55082

© Timothy Remus, 2006

The information in this book is true and complete to the best of our knowledge. All recommendations are made without any guarantee on the part of the author or publisher, who also disclaim any liability incurred in connection with the use of this data or specific details.

We recognize that some words, model names and designations, for example, mentioned herein are the property of the trademark holder. We use them for identification purposes only. This is not an official publication.

ISBN number: 1-929133-28-6

Printed and bound in China

Professional Airbrush Techniques with Vince Goodeve

Acknowledgements

This book is dedicated in Loving Memory of my Grandfather Roland Dennis Goodeve, 1912-1999, sign painter and artist from the early 50's who was an inspiration to me and kept the craft alive well into his 80's, he still guides my every brush stroke.

I would like to use this space to thank all the people who made this book possible. From the many talented bike builders who supplied me with beautiful curving steel canvas, as well as the guys who trust me with their own four-wheel sheet metal, to the Hamsters U.S.A for their friendship and for broadening my perspective in the custom motorcycle industry.

I hope this book will help young up-and-coming artists, as well as provide some new perspectives to the seasoned veterans. As I grew up there were very few reference books on custom paint and airbrush work, except, of course, the legendry John Kozmoski's stuff. Certainly there was not anyone to show it to you step by step, they all treated it like it was a big secret. Usually my curiosity was rewarded with a beer bottle hurled from the dark studio.

Maybe this book will address that issue and join the other excellent books on the subject today. All I know is, it's a learning process that never really ends. I am always finding new or more efficient ways to accomplish things. So take the advice that I offer in this book and run with it, nothing is more rewarding than to see my influence in other artist's work.

Many things inspire us in our life, for me it was hot rods and motorcycles. I was always hanging around the local A&W waiting to see the midnight drag races for pink slips. Those brooding monsters always gave me chills, I wanted to emulate their glistening candy paint and mural jobs. As for my artistic inspiration, it grew from cover art on books and magazines featuring, Boris Vallejo, Frank Frazetta, and at present Luis Royo and Todd Mcfarlane. Wherever you find it, let it penetrate your head and soul and drive you to new goals.

Special thanks to Tim Remus for his extreme professionalism and patience putting this whole thing together. Also to Steve Aungers from Bear Air for his support over the last three years, Andy Anderson, a friend and confidant (I'm his biggest fan, but don't tell him) also PPG for their awesome products. The guys at KC Auto Paint and Supplies for hookin' me up with all the paint supplies I needed when I was in Boise, Idaho doing Devils Playground. Dan Metzger for always being there to lend a hand, and Fox Harley-Davidson for all the tear downs and reassemblies, and their awesome crates. Linda Turner for all her hard work for the past four years in helping get the bikes ready for paint. Craig and Kathy from Scenic City Automotive for keeping us supplied even on weekends and after hours.

Last but not least my wife and business partner, Lisa, without whom this book literally could not have happened.

"Wear your respirators and Paint Everything"

From The Publisher

The first time I met Vince Goodeve was in Sturgis, during a photo shoot for a pair of custom motorcycles, I quickly learned that his tough-guy exterior hides a generous and friendly interior.

His friendly nature means he's always willing to share what he knows about paint and painting. Like master painter Jon Kosmoski, Vince never seems to tire of painting projects. Burn-out isn't part of his vocabulary or personality. Vince seems as excited about the project currently in his shop as he was about the paint or graphics job he did ten years ago. To get Vince to discuss an old or new paint job, or some new airbrush technique, is one of the easiest things in the world.

Combine twenty years of experience with Vince's personality and you have the ideal person to teach airbrushing. Though this may be Vince's first book, it's hardly the first time he's shared his skills with a wider audience. Vince Goodeve airbrushing seminars started under the *Airbrush Action* umbrella more than five years ago. Since teaching that first class, Vince, with help from his wife Lisa, has gone on to teach his own airbrushing seminars.

For all those airbrush enthusiasts who can't travel to Vince's shop in Owen Sound, Ontario, we offer you this Vince Goodeve book. Making a good book can be difficult without the right ingredients. In this case, we've taken twenty years of painting experience, combined with five years of teaching seminars, to bring you what I hope is the printed equivalent of a weekend with Vince.

From metal preparation to design, from color choice to tips on mixing and reducing paint, Vince shares with you what he's learned in all these years of custom paint and airbrush work.

Vince writes the way he talks, with lots of enthusiasm and plenty of slang. In putting the book together we've tried to leave all the "Vince-isms" intact, so that what you get is the real McCoy, the undiluted Vince. Airbrush wisdom from a man who truly has a huge amount of knowledge to share.

Thus, it's my great pleasure to bring you 144 pages of Vince Goodeve.

Timothy Remus

Chapter One

Shop Setup

Clean, Efficient and Safe

The goal for your shop setup is two fold. One is the business end. This includes the show room, signage, parking, your vehicle, advertising and all the rest. This is the face your client sees first as they first approach. Secondly, and equally important, is your setup of all the equipment and space that you need to create your end product. It's important to use the square footage efficiently. For example, don't put your polishing area next to your prepping for paint stations. Common sense

yes, but I've seen it done. Put as much thought into the planning and design as you do the final execution.

Another aspect is safety. You have to deal with ventilation, disposal of toxic materials and fire hazards. These are all things that can really haunt you if not addressed in the initial setup and planning. This chapter goes over each facet briefly as I'm sure there's probably another book here if I went into every detail on each one.

The front door to the business end of our company. Our sign can easily be read from the adjacent highway.

Whether you choose to make your showroom look like Caesars palace or something a little more humble, it needs to be professional, with lots of your work on display and great lighting. Have your portfolios laid out in an organized manner. A nice choice of color samples and other sales tools are imperative. You want your client to be comfortable, but also impressed.

Here is a view of our second area. We keep the lighting warm in the showroom and spot-light our work for real sizzle.

Color Usage

First of all, this isn't an attempt to condense color theory into a fairly brief side bar. There are entire books, and even lives, dedicated to it's explanation and theories. Rather, I'm just going to give you some of my ideas and principles I use regularly and that I find effective in improving the overall look of a project.

My number one principal is "light to show dark and dark to show light." This principle is the first thing I consider when doing my black and white compositions. I often use dramatic lighting, which pushes either lighter areas forward with dark areas behind or just the opposite. The same thing applies in my more graphic jobs like flames and vectors, pick colors that contrast each other well.

Flow is another thing that I think about, especially in motorcycle or vehicle art. You should really be conscious of the geometry of the sheet metal you're painting and work with the shapes rather than against them. A good design can really slam an already low vehicle or stretch an already long chopper.

There are practices I try to avoid, particularly in my murals and imagery. Number one here is the over use of straight black, it tends to look unnatural and is easily overdone. It also reproduces poorly, creating dramatic dark spots when scanned, these often appear as a separate color all together.

I tend to lean toward dark purples and browns for my darkest areas. I also like to knock back the chroma (intensity) of a color with its complimentary color rather than tint with black, it creates a more vibrant overall look to your design. For example, if I'm working in yellow/oranges or red/oranges, I add a small amount of blue or purple to buffer them slightly and reduce their chroma (intensity). Then for the darkest shadows I'll add a little green which gives me an almost-black color that still smacks

When it comes to my own work I much prefer to work with transparent rather than opaque colors. And I don't use very much true black.

Color Usage

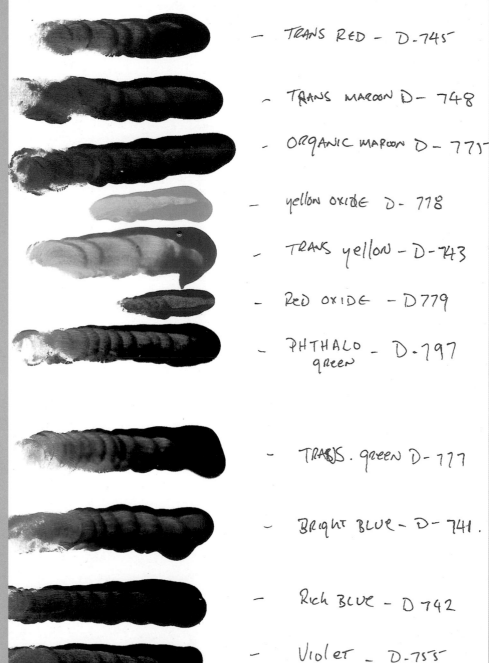

- TRANS RED - D-745
- TRANS MAROON D- 748
- ORGANIC MAROON D - 775
- Yellow OXIDE D- 778
- TRANS Yellow - D-743
- RED OXIDE - D779
- PHTHALO - D-797
  green
- TRANS. green D-777
- BRIGHT BLUE - D- 741.
- Rich BLUE - D-742
- Violet - D-755

Here are the main colors of my palette that I build everything from. They are PPG's Global Basecoat Toners.

of its original shades and harmonies.

Since I work predominantly in transparent colors this method works well for me.

I like to mix shades or colors on my piece as I go. To elaborate, if I'm looking for a greenish image I'll do a lot of my work in bluish tones. Then I apply a light wash of yellow, which gives me a nice vibrant green look in the end.

I do use black as a tint in monochromatic work or in building nice neutral grays. For example: a little blue, a little red, a dash of white and a hint of black gives me a nice cool grey. Now however, we are working in opaque, something I very rarely do in my motorcycle art.

I would suggest taking a course on color theory or reading a few good books. I've got a whole library of books about color. Color is a subject you can study for a lifetime, a subject that still gives a rush when you find a new way to use, apply or mix color. I tell people, "Find your style and run with it, because the only person you have to impress is yourself."

A view from our office space where our clients sit during consultations, as well as pay the bills.

Work Space #1, the booth.
The spray booth is your largest invest-ment and space eater (unless you plan to farm out this work) so position it in an area that allows maximum access to the other useful spaces. If you plan to operate in a commercial space take into account hidden costs for all the inspec-tion and operating codes. Remember to budget for removal of waste and used paint and thinners. Booths vary greatly in price, the most important things is to maintain the filters and keep the booth clean.

Work Space #2, the mixing area.
This is where you concoct your paint formulas, and store reducers and other products. I also like to keep all my painting equipment (spray guns and cleaning station) and my waste removal stuff here. Strictly enforce NO SMOK-ING in your shop. I've seen a body shop burn to the ground in 30 minutes. Don't allow any form of spark near this area including welders and grinders. You need to dispose properly of used thinners and paints, either contract a pick up service, share with another shop, or take to an approved facility.

Workspace # 3, prep and bodywork. This area can be high tech or simple. Just make sure you have good lighting with lots of shelves and work benches, as well as cabinets for your tools and materials.

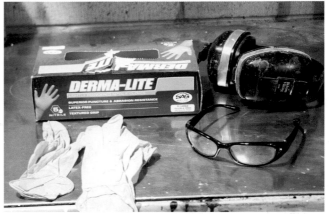

Health and safety issues. Wear gloves so paint chemicals don't get to your bloodstream though the skin. Eyewear is a must for any kind of grinding. Use ear protection whenever you use noisy power tools.

This is a close up of my air brushing station. Always messy, and always functional. The flexible ducting is connected to a filter and an exhaust fan.

Workspace # 4, polishing area. Keep this space isolated, to isolate the mess and also to keep body shop dust or metal particles from sneaking into the paint area to ruin a paint job.

Workspace # 5, design and airbrush station. This area should be separate from the rest of the shop's noise and distractions. I mix up my lighting between fluorescents and incandescent to give a nice balance. Allow for 50% more room than you can imagine.

More health and safety issues. The products we use are deadly. Wear your particulate mask when sanding, your charcoal mask when mixing and airbrushing. By all means use a fresh air system and paint suit when spraying bases, clear, candy and primers.

Chapter Two

Prepping the Metal Canvas

Make it Smooth, Really Smooth

I think it's a good idea to add a chapter about getting a bike ready for paint. From the time it arrives at our door, to the final stages before the art work and basecoats begin. Whether you do this stage yourself or not, it's knowledge that will help you see the amount of work that goes into the process. This stage can ultimately make or break the longevity of your paint job. Obviously, to do it right takes way more time than to do it quick and dirty. The hours you spend on preparation are thus reflected in the price of the job. My methods, explained in this chapter, take longer, but they're worth it as the end product will definitely withstand the test of time.

This is a story of a bikes' birth from rough sheet metal and welds to a smooth, pressure tested, (to assure no gas leaks) rolling piece of art. Ashley Ranson

Material List

- Small hammer and chisel
- Angle grinder 80 grit
- Porting tool
- Access to professional sandblaster
- Quality body filler (Rage or equivalents)
- Light weight polyester filler
- Direct to metal primer or epoxy
- Industrial tank or rad sealer
- 40,80,120,180, grit sand paper
- 600-800 grit wet sand paper
- Various spreaders and body shop tools
- Professional spray booth & respiratory equipment

In this first frame you see the bike "just born" when it comes to me. I re-assemble it as far as I can to get a feel for the overall look, and as an overall check of fitment issues before starting on the finish and prep work.

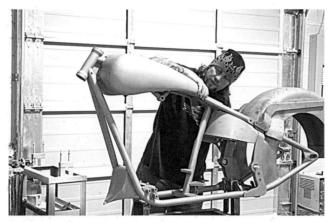

I am checking for clearances, and any high spots that may have to be ground off. Just giving it a once over before beginning the huge task of making this pile of sheet metal as smooth as glass.

Using an old screwdriver and the palm of my hand as a hammer, I'm removing more mig welding splatter. The splatter can show up later as little bumps under the basecoat that can't be removed.

Next, I clean off any welding slag that was left behind. Also, notice the entire frame and all its parts have been sand blasted. This will help the body filler adhere to the metal.

In this frame you see that I am disassembling the bike to get ready for the journey ahead.

Now, I make a template so I know where the seat goes, this way I can work my designs around the seat space.

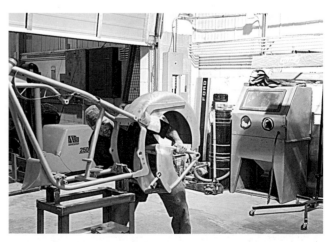

Here I'm removing the swing arm and the last components prior to the body work phase.

This shot shows me the grinding any of the areas that I don't like, areas that might be a problem before I start the body work.

I hit it with 40 grit sand paper, some guys use a block on complex curves like this, but I prefer to use my hand with folded paper. I'm kinda just going by feel.

Here I've got the back of the fender full of body filler, mixed and applied as evenly possible to make up for the high and low spots in the sheet metal.

See the evil pin holes and air pockets. Sometimes when you are spreading Bondo over a large area, air gets trapped. Open up any big holes and apply a thin second coat.

The body file or cheese grater allows me to cut off a lot of mud fast, concentrating on shape and contour as opposed to smoothness in this early stage. You can start shaping before the mud is fully set up.

I'm spreading the second, thinner coat of Bondo to fill up all those pin holes and achieve the surface or roundness that I want. Notice how I take my time and spread it really carefully.

After applying the second coat of filler I finished the section in 80 Grit paper. This is how I do the whole bike, section, by section, by section.

Be sure to blow any dust off between coats of Bondo or else you will trap dust in there and cause problems later.

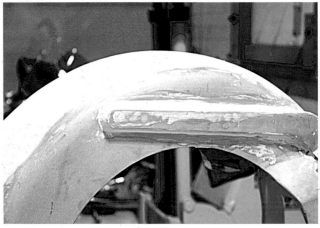

For this next section I use my fingers to squish the Bondo tight against the metal work, keeping out any air bubbles.

Don't be afraid to grind a little hear and there, it makes your job a little easier in the end.

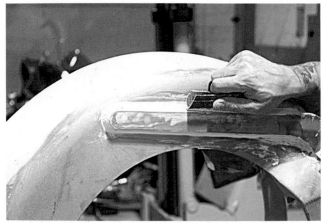

It is always helpful to bend the paper in weird and wondrous shapes when you are molding a custom motorcycle.

Here I'm molding the frame into the gas tank fitting so that it will be smooth and seamless. This requires moving the tank on and off the bike many times to make sure the margins are correct in this area.

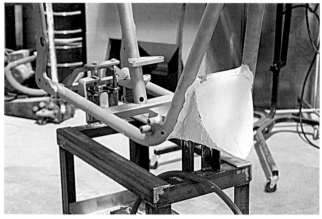

Here's my first pass of filler on the spoiler, or air dam which ever you prefer, the idea is to make it seamless where it meets the frame.

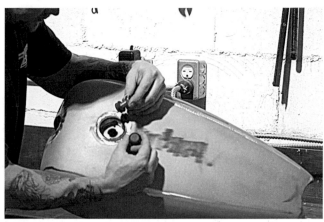

This is the first step in sealing a tank. The hard part is finding ways to prevent the sealer-goop from running out once you pour it in. I use old rubber plugs and gas caps to seal the tank and cross-over tubes.

My second pass of Bondo on the air dam, I'm being careful to keep it tight to the sheet metal. The high spots are my guide, I try to keep them just below the surface of the filler.

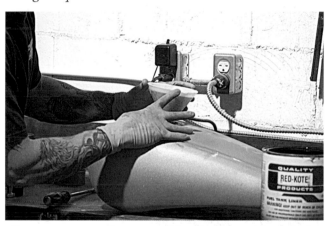

Time to pour in four cups of Red Coat tank sealer. Before you pour it in make sure you rinse the tank out with thinners to eliminate any oils inside, and make sure the inside is dry. Note the gloves.

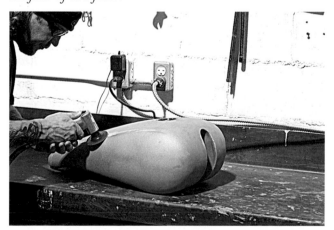

Here I'm knocking down the high spots on the tank and cleaning it up.

The first order of business is to rotate the tank slowly to every possible angle to try and get an initial coating of the liquid on the entire inside surface. I'll usually do this for about 15 minutes.

After about 15 minutes of sloshing around, open up the bottom plug and drain out the excess. This allows the remaining liquid in the tank to dry faster.

Continue turning the tank, a turn every 15 minutes or so, in every possible direction, Sometimes I'll look in there with a flash light to see how to the drying process is going.

The heat lamps can be used for more than drying paint and Bondo.

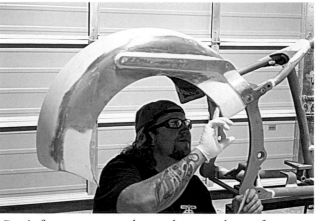

Don't forget to get underneath everywhere, if you know where it is, everyone else does too. So get underneath into all the weird places and get them all cleaned up.

You have to get filler into all those small and awkward places and there's no better way to do it than with your fingers. Gloves would be a good idea.

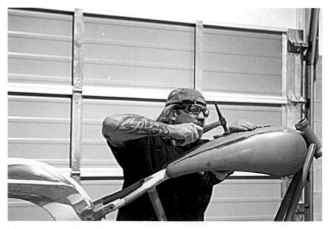

Don't be afraid to use other tools to help massage the metal. High spots need to be addressed, remember to keep them just below the original margins and don't load it up with tons of filler.

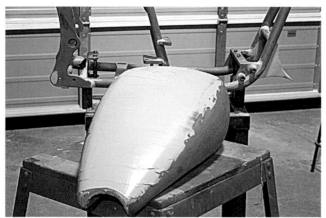

The initial smear of filler should look like this. I tend to use perpendicular initial strokes with the filler and finish with horizontal strokes when I am spreading, to emulate the shape of the surface.

Now I can see the fruits of my labor and begin to picture in my mind what the canvas will look like. As part of this process, I start to picture the design for the paint. It's one benefit to my hands-on approach.

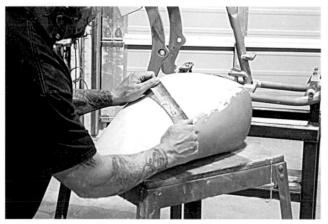

Using a cheese file, I attack the filler before it is completely cured. Timing is everything, if you start too soon you will rip the filler off, and if you begin too late you're shaping a cement-like mixture.

Don't forget the inside and bottom of the tank. Clean it all up and match up the margins where the tank meets other parts of the bike.

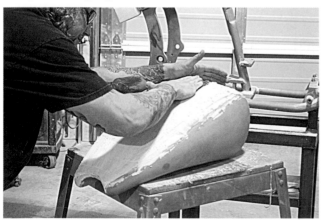

Back to the 40 grit paper, shaping it with my hand. Keep in mind you want the surface as straight as an arrow. Using my hand without a block I can feel the compound curves more accurately.

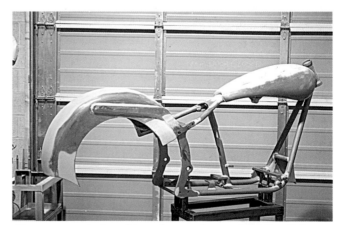

You can see it is taking shape, the underside of the tank is done and fitted to the margins, I just have to mold the rest of the little welds.

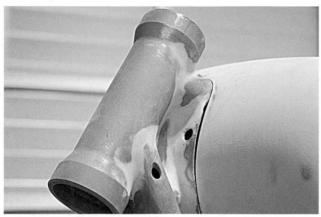

Here you see the neck area with the tight fitment between the tank and the chassis. Be sure to keep all cable and wire channels open and free of filler.

The next 3 or 4 frames show me detailing the bottom of the bike. Pay attention to detail underneath, this is what separates the amateurs from the pros, believe me people are looking at these areas.

Sometimes you will find flipping the frame over makes life a lot easier. It's incredible how much you'll miss by skipping this step. The bike really isn't finished.

With the frame upside down, I pay attention to the underside of the air dam and forward control attachment points.

After 2-3 days of molding you will find your hand starts to give out and you use various things like bandages, or tape, to keep body fluids from oozing out on your work.

Just slugging it out under the frame, catching all the last little imperfections before I flip it over and reassemble the bike. By the way, I'm still at the 40 grit paper stage at this point.

You have to work both the inside and outside of the fender, everywhere people can see. Sand the areas, make sure everything is flat, because people will be looking, details count.

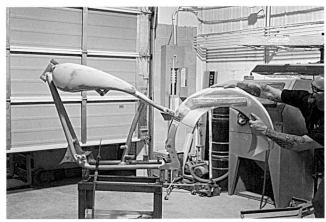

Using long aggressive strokes with your sand paper helps to get the long contours straight.

I go over the bike in 80, then 120 grit respectably, and catch anything that was missed earlier. At this point I'm getting ready to primer the bike.

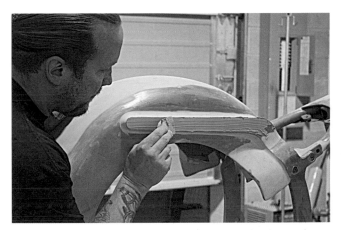

Just when you think you are done, you find another spot. So after a few hours of pin holes and final things, I 'm ready to throw it in the booth and apply primer. Spot putty can be used for the pin holes.

Using 120 grit paper really knocks down the edges where filler meets steel. Some guys prefer to leave it rough and lay primer on, then sand and lay more primer on. I like to get it as smooth as I can with filler before reaching for the primer.

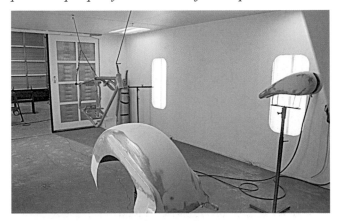

I will apply three good coats of PPG DTM primer with about a ten minute splash-off between coats. The idea is to get a nice uniform layering of paint.

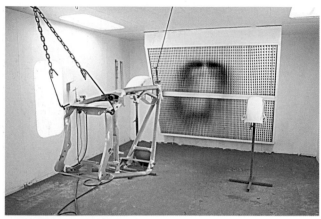

You will notice that the various methods of holding the components vary greatly from job to job. That's why having a mig welder handy to build your various fixtures is a definite bonus.

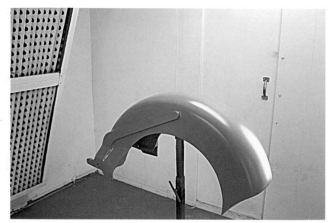

Here is the rear fender after priming. I use PPG's DTM primers as they fill great and have super adhesion properties.

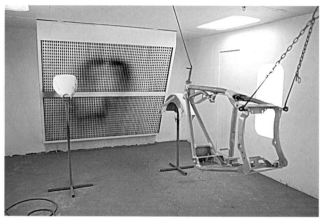

I like to suspend my frames from heavy duty eyelets in the top of my booth. That way I can get at it from all angles when I'm spraying.

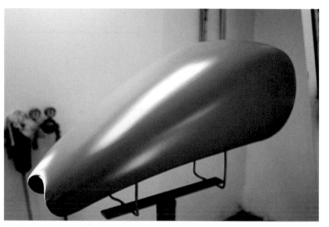

The fuel tank after 3 coats of primer, be sure to allow time for the product to flash off adequately between coats, or you'll trap reducers between the layers and your job will be more prone to showing sand-scratches.

Spraying the primer, yee ha (time to give my digits a break). Check out my space suit! Really important, actually by law I have to wear the correct equipment when spraying.

The booth is a must. First for your health and safety, as primer and most paints are extremely toxic. The other big advantage is dust control.

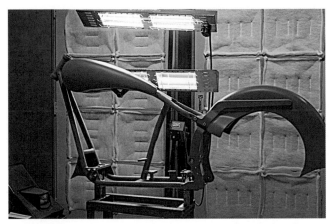

With the primer applied, we are going to bake the primer with a short-wave infrared light. I will do this as a two-step process.

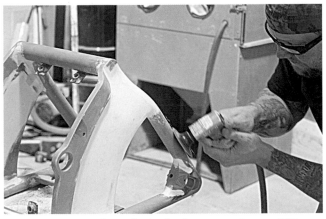

Here I am grinding down high spots prior to filling the tube areas of the swing arm. Never grind excessively, especially the welds, or you will weaken the structure.

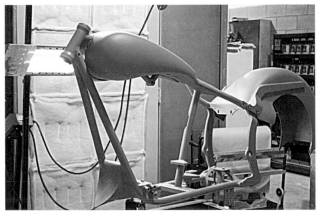

To make sure that the paint is fully cured I reposition the lights once before flipping the bike to bake the other side. I want the paint fully cured so there is no movement, or sinking of the filler later.

Even the smallest nuts and brackets are molded. Be sure an area like this is free of debris and mig weld slag before you start with the filler.

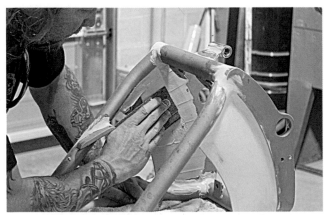

Some of the other components arrived after the frame was primered, so I repeated the mud work sequence seen on the rest of the bike parts.

A heavy application of filler ensures I'll have enough material to mold the shape into the frame.

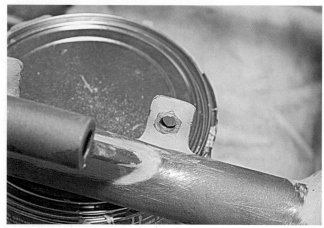

This is the detail area after rough sanding. I've also chased the threads with a tap so I will be sure to have easy assembly later.

I am tearing at the Bondo with 40 grit paper shaping it before adding a second coat of filler. Body work can be a real workout.

Here is the swing arm ready for primer, I'll need to manufacture a method to hang this in the spray booth.

Another coat of filler on the large curved fender. I like to get it as complete and smooth as possible, talk about a huge smear.

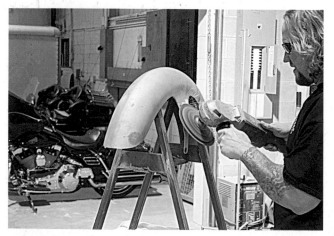

The front fender needed a little attention with my large format grinder. I just had to zing off a few high spots.

Once I've done the filler work to my satisfaction, up to a 120 grit level, I blow it off and it's ready for primer, and I'm ready for a shower.

Here you see the swing arm, oil tank, inner fender, front fender, two head lights, a set of custom bars, engine mounts, bushings, oil tank mount, engine mounts, secondary mounts and axle nut covers. I'm ready to switch to the next phase, which is sanding everything with 180 grit paper. At this point you will be glad to put down the 40, 80 and 120 grit paper you were using and grab on to some nice soft 180 paper. It will feel good after the five days of punishment on your skin.

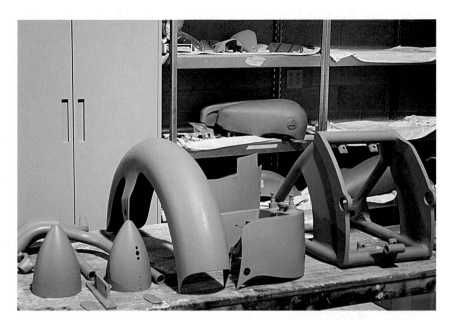

My initial goal was to get everything straight and smooth. For the secondary stage I want to take it one step higher, eliminating any small minor fluctuations in the surface, getting it flat and smooth by using blocks. I've applied a guide coat using a little black base (a contrasting color) misted lightly on top of the primer. After you sand the primer with a block, you will see the remaining guide coat in the low spots.

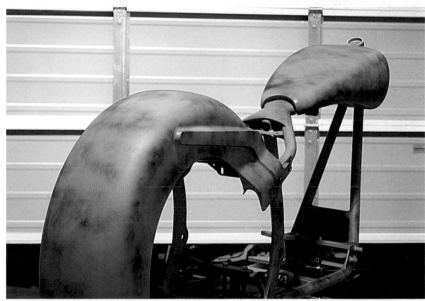

Here you can see some of the low spots that are revealed from the guide coat. The parts that are dark are lows. So you keep sanding until it is completely smooth. I continue this process through the entire bike.

Here I'm working on the bike with a soft flexible sanding pad and a piece of 180 grit paper. The darker color is called a guide coat because the remaining dark paint will guide you to the low spots.

Before and after, a small imperfection on the rear fender strut. Small little areas like this can be quickly repaired with two-part spot putty. It's faster and easier than mixing up a new batch of body filler.

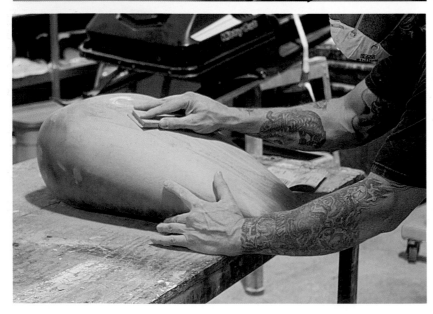

You have to keep sanding with the 180 until all the guide coat is gone, or you decide to deal with low spots with spot putty, or more primer.

FINISHING THE PREPARATION

Once the bike is all wet sanded with 800 grit, you're ready to rock and roll. You can see it is quite an extensive job getting a full molded custom paint job ready for paint and airbrush work. Key to success is patience and a keen eye to find all the flaws and mistakes. Because no matter how good your finished paint job or art work is, it will show poorly if the prep work isn't perfect. No matter how stunning your airbrush work is, it must be applied over a perfectly prepared surface. If there are flaws others *will* see them. The prep work is everything baby.

THE GOODEVE METAL PREP SEQUENCE

- Finish all welding and metal work
- Apply the first coat of body filler
- Sand with 40 grit
- Apply second coat of filler
- Sand with 40, 80 then 120 grit
- Apply 3 or 4 coats of good two-part primer
- Apply a light contrasting guide coat
- Sand with 180 grit
- Use spot putty on remaining low spots
- Apply another 3 to 4 coats of primer
- Apply another guide coat
- Final sanding with 600 to 800 grit wet depending on the job

In closing, the methods that I've show you for molding a bike and preparing it for final paint are the methods I was taught years ago. By no means is my way the only way to do this. I know as fast as you can rip a piece of sand paper in half, someone will contradict me because their way is probably better in their minds. I can only say this has been working well for me for the last twenty-some years and I have never had any problems. I've tried to give you an overview on how Goodeve studios gets a show bike ready, how we prep the metal canvas.

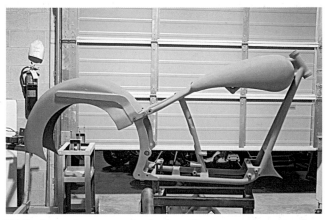

Well, there she is, ready for another 3 good coats of primer. After a final scuff with 800 we will get to the artwork. Be sure to let the primer cure fully before moving on to the next step.

Use a dry rag to keep things clean as you do the final wet sand. As you wipe up the water, do a careful inspection. You should have one flat smooth, surface ready for paint.

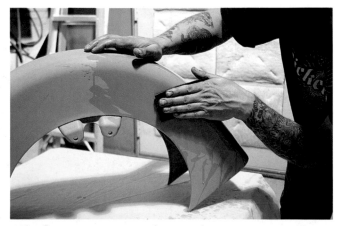

The last step is wet sanding with 800 grit wet after another guide coat. You have to go over every inch to make sure it is absolutely flawless.

Chapter Three

Nine Dragons

Bronze Dragon against a Sea of Silver and Black

To start this project I gave the entire bike a nice basecoat of dark silver. The artwork, the nice bronze tones set against the dark silver, should have real rich medieval feel to it when it's finished. In creating the dragon I wanted the images to be vibrant and clean. To achieve this I avoided adding black as a tint to any of my artwork. Instead I continually darkened my colors by adding a small touch of the color's compliment to the darkest shadowed areas to create a pseudo-black.

A look at the assembled bike, with the cleared and polished tank. The beautiful studio lighting plays up the subtle color changes. Ashley Ranson

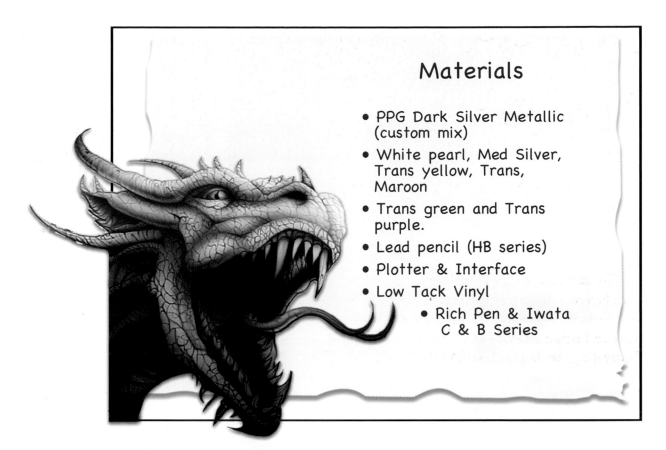

Materials

- PPG Dark Silver Metallic (custom mix)
- White pearl, Med Silver, Trans yellow, Trans, Maroon
- Trans green and Trans purple.
- Lead pencil (HB series)
- Plotter & Interface
- Low Tack Vinyl
- Rich Pen & Iwata C & B Series

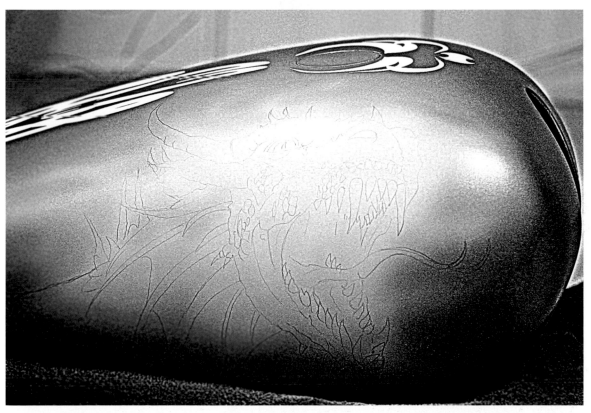

I lightly sketched out my dragon face with a lead pencil. At this stage I've already blown in a bit of a background - white pearl and slightly lighter silvers - to start working on. To start I made up a nice bronzy mixture, which is transparent maroon and transparent red with a little transparent yellow. Then I start playing around with the colors to build the first image.

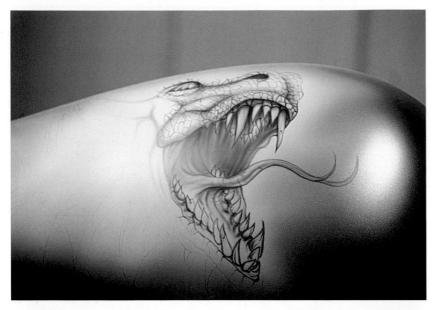

I start establishing the shapes with my mixture of color. I am not too concerned about the deep dark areas inside the mouth. These areas are going to be very briefed in because I am going to be coming in with progressively darker tones later. Just use suggestive areas to make sure that you have something to play off later in the shadow regions. Basically, I am just trying to get a feel for the color and how it is going to work with the overall design of the entire bike at this stage.

I continue working on the subject adding texture and making a game plan to give it more dimension as I go. But first I want to finish the entire dragons face, and what ever else I want to put in there in the one color - so that I can come back and work it evenly in darker tones and progressively push the shadows deeper.

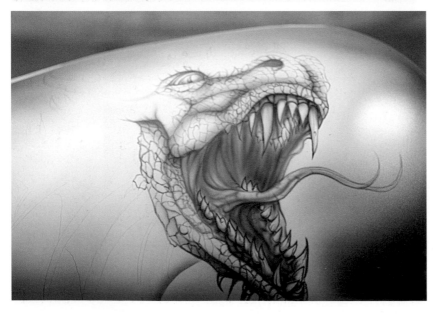

At this stage I'm building the shapes and adding interesting pointy objects to the dragon to make him a little more vicious. Working on the body will come next.

I progress, working in the same color I started with. I'm working on the lighter details filling out any of the scales, getting ready to start coming in to some darker colors. But at this stage I keep it very monochromatic and try not to get too excited about darkening up the darkest areas, that's my job in the next little while.

I add a few drops of purple to my mix, to start knocking back the shadows. I'm pushing in the areas I want to appear deeper and recessed. I use these colors on top of the existing rusty tones to build a rich deep shadow area until the teeth start to stand out, that will give them a realistic look.

You now see how effective these darker shades are as a way to add depth and form to the subject. I have also added a light wash of transparent red into the mouth and eye area to give it a more interesting fleshy kind of membrane look. I continue working in this manner balancing color and enhancing detail in the next few steps.

31

By adding the complement color green, to the reddish tone that I have now, it will knock it back and make almost a mock black. In its darkest areas I will use this color, like the deepest part of the nostril and recesses of the throat area, and perhaps some places in the eye. Be very careful with this color - you can over do it

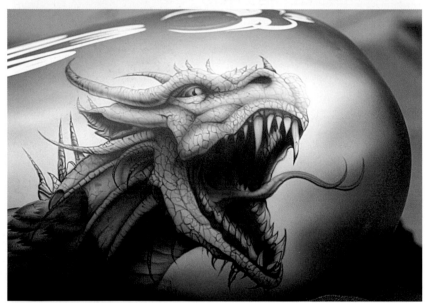

Using pure transparent purple, I go into the deepest and final shadow areas knocking them back to their completion. I also use the purple to adjust any points that seem inconsistent as far as gradient shadows go.

I go over with some transparent red in some areas to try to make it look a little more like fleshy membranes, and then I take a little transparent yellow and warm up some of the transitions between my darks and my lights.

This shows the completed portion of the dragon that will be continued through the rest of the bike. Notice that the highlights in the right areas drag everything forward.

A detailed shot of the mouth area, a little bit of saliva lends action and movement to the creature. I also hit the edges of the scales and bring forward any of my dark spikes that extend into the dark areas of my design.

A nice detailed shot of the eye, you always have to make sure to put the soul into the eye. It should look like it is looking right through you, so realistic you swear it's going to blink. Keep in mind there are several ways to make highlights, just remember they should originate from your main light source.

Chapter Four

Boxing Thru Time

Art as History

This bike was a blast! Especially since I'm a huge fan of pugilism, as well as being a participant of the sport for many years. The owner, Bill Minus, wanted to pay tribute to the great sport on his bike. I decided to start by lacing the whole thing up like a giant boxing glove. The hook would be to highlight some of the most famous fights in history and to have fight cards here and there to reflect important issues in history relevant to that particular fight. Let's get ready to rummmmble!!!

Here is a shot of the bike outside our shop after the client made his first spring ride. The transparent colors rock in the sun, and the balance of the elements create a nice flow to the artwork.

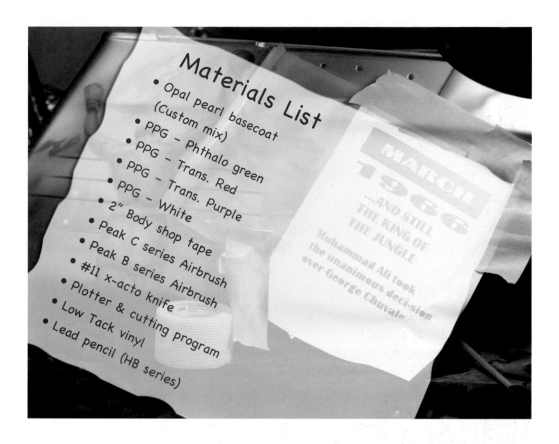

Materials List

- Opal pearl basecoat (Custom mix)
- PPG – Phthalo green
- PPG – Trans. Red
- PPG – Trans. Purple
- PPG – White
- 2" Body shop tape
- Peak C series Airbrush
- Peak B series Airbrush
- #11 X-acto knife
- Plotter & cutting program
- Low Tack vinyl
- Lead pencil (HB series)

MARCH 1966 ...AND STILL THE KING OF THE JUNGLE Muhammad Ali took the unanimous decision over George Chuvalo

I'll take you through one segment of the bike, otherwise it would encompass an entire book to cover everything. I begin, like I usually do, by creating a luminous area in white on which to build the image. Since we are using transparent colors, you'll need that white to pop out the rich radiance of the tones.

I begin to sketch my figures, in this case Muhammad Ali standing over George Chevelo. Remember to keep the detail light, leave that for the airbrush stage. I'm just looking for the major components.

Add the referee using the same tones as the boxer. The look we're going for is a photo you might find in your grandparents' living room. I fade to nothing on the right to leave room for the fight card I'm dropping in.

Using phthalo green (D-777) and trans red (D-745) approximately 10% green and 90% red, I create a sienna color to suggest an aged look to the entire design.

Adding a little purple I darken up my shadows, giving the darks more punch and creating additional detail. Notice I work right over the body lines in the saddle bag.

Working off my reference picture, I develop the form and musculature of Cassius Clay, an old photo-exposed-to-elements look.

Needing a hard line to represent the edge of the ring, I place 2 inch body shop tape strategically as a template. Softly I suggest the crowd figures. Keeping the figures out of focus just like a camera would.

Remove the tape, and give the ring a little life. Note the soda cups and all the rest. By taping off the crowd we have created a great area of light to represent the middle ground of our piece.

I add the ropes free hand as well as any other embellishments. Check out how the ropes being placed over the softer crowd in the background creates an illusion of depth. I also darken up the mist in the distance that I use to tie everything together, like a dream sequence from a movie-.

White camera flashes and mist complete this segment. Highlights on the figures help cement the old photo look, I sometimes over do them just for that reason. Once again the mist is a good element to plug into as a way to carry the design through the rest of the bike.

Using my plotter I design and cut out my headlines for the discarded newspaper clips. I place it directly on the base coat and make sure to add extra 2" tape on the side to protect the rest of the art from creeping overspray!

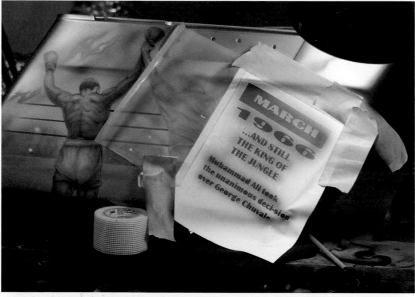

I spray the lettering lightly with my original sepia color. Be sure to get enough color on for good contrast against the underlying basecoat color.

Using the darker mixture (adding a little purple) I antique the letters by spraying dark and light transitions throughout.

Remove the vinyl template and pick out the insides of the letters. Leaving excess vinyl now would be a problem after the clear. Also look for left over adhesive from the vinyl, wipe this off gently with DX 320.

I take off the tape and tie everything together with mist and color. In some areas I go extremely dark, almost like fire damage. Also, a light mist of purple in key areas adds a subtle fatness to our color scheme.

Using 2 inch body shop masking tape I create the outside edge of the newspaper and spray my white in varying degrees of density at a 45 degree to suggest undulation in the paper.

Right side saddle bag view, you can see the victorious boxer as well as 2 fight cards for that particular era in fight history. Notice the antiquing on the back of the bag.

I then add a shadow in the hollows of the ripples we created in the last step. For this I go back to the seine mixture we made earlier for the figures.

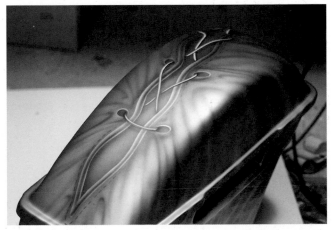

The right saddle bag lid. The laces and rich shadow in the transparent color will rock outside in the natural light after the clearcoat process.

This is the knockout fairing. Capturing the stop action was a challenge. The exploding sweat and swollen distorted features of the faces (the result of the impact) was key.

Muhammad Ali vs Joe Frazer knockout on the left side tank. The curious poses of the human figure in action always amaze me. It's almost as if they are made of rubber and the bones act unnaturally especially in the unconscious fellow ready for his brief nap on the canvas. In this case, it's a canvas you don't paint upon.

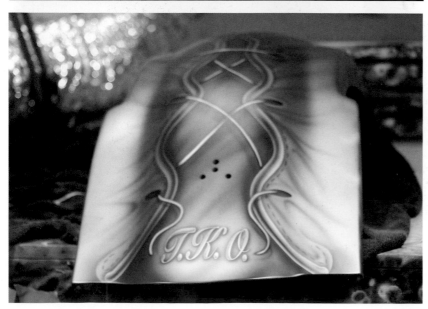

A shot of the rear fender prior to clear coat and reassembly. The bike adopted the name T.K.O (Technical Knock Out), and I think it fits. The script adds a touch of class to a brutal subject just like world championship boxers who wear tuxedos.

Front fairing after clearcoat and assembly. The natural light and clear coat followed by the polishing process adds ton's of depth and brings all the transparent colors together.

Here's T.K.O. Gassed up and ready to rock. It's always kool to see your art come alive and roll off into the distance.

Chapter Five

Burning Money

The Wages of Sin

This project bike was built in Springfield, Illinois. The owner, Sean Watts, wanted to portray the slippery slope of greed and narcissism. So my main figure in the center of the tank suggests the eventual destiny of the souls who worship wealth.

My plan is to use a unique color palette for the paint work, as well as incredible detail to pull this off successfully.

Here is a close up of the Demon featured in the main mural on the top of the tank, and it shows how I use dark and light to push the forms of the figure forward.

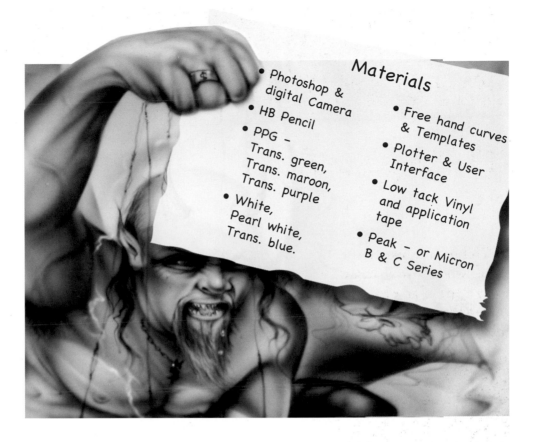

Materials

- Photoshop & digital Camera
- HB Pencil
- PPG –
  Trans. green,
  Trans. maroon,
  Trans. purple
- White,
  Pearl white,
  Trans. blue.

- Free hand curves & Templates
- Plotter & User Interface
- Low tack Vinyl and application tape
- Peak – or Micron B & C Series

Finding a demon to pose for me proved to be a challenge, so I decided to create my own. Using a digital camera and my Photoshop program I altered my model to a position I could work with, then embellished him so I could use it in my design.

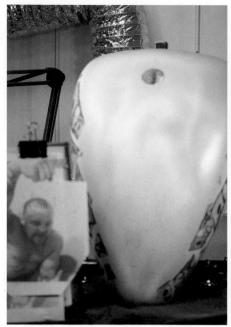

Using a light pencil I start by sketching my design onto a misty white background, which gives me a nice canvas to build my colors on.

Using PPG toners I mix trans-green (D-777), a couple drops of trans maroon (D-748), and about 10% trans purple (D-755) to create an organic dark green. I check it by doing a smear on white paper.

Working the darkest parts of my piece at the bottom I establish my light and shadow as well as form. I want this piece to look very cartoonish, so I almost completely finish the detail as I move along.

I move up the thigh, being sure to have a nice dark area to pop that lighter skull into the foreground.

Working the torso, be sure to mix up your line work as well as place soft airbrush work next to crisp lines, to give your project better dynamics.

Rendering the face. Notice how much lighter my technique is in the top portions and shadows. It's easy to make the features way too dark.

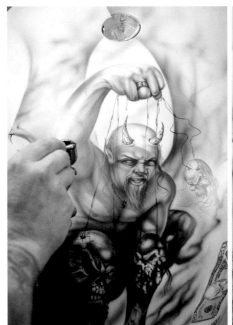

Using freehand curves as templates, and soft hand techniques, I create a suggestion of wings behind the fiend.

Here is our boy with all the dark contrast adjusted. Step back occasionally from your design and make sure all your mid-tones and darks relate to each other in balance and as a whole.

I add white and grey highlights to tie everything together, keeping in mind my light source. It's also a great time to soften up edges on the highlight side. I also start to drag my mist into the other elements for easy plug in later.

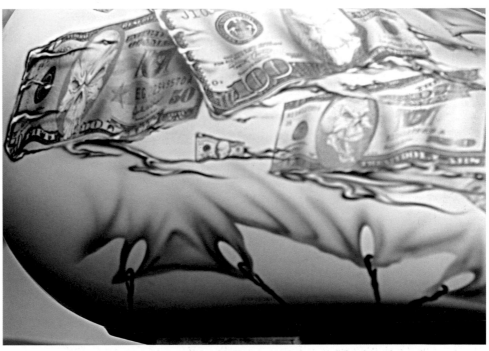

Here's the second element, created by endless templates and freehand work, and an ink release process that gives me the flow through the bike profile. I've replaced the original presidents with skulls and altered the perspective of the bills for extra depth. Note the beginning to the third element which is the stretched parchment.

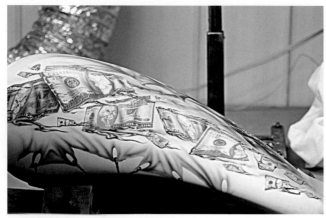

I created the stretched parchment look using freehand templates. Just find a shape to suit your need and spray away leaving a nice clean hard, or semi-hard, edge to work from.

Using pencil, I sketch my design for the skulls, I like a light HB series lead. Look for balance, and try to place dark areas next to the templates so there will be adequate contrast for them to show up.

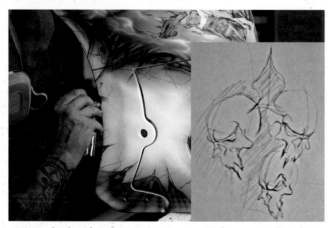

A quick sketch of my next image, I keep my sketches very simple saving my energy for the actual execution. A blast of white and white pearl will provide the basis upon which to start my design.

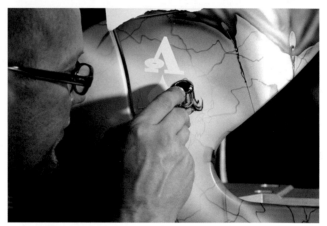

Using my original greenish mixture that I did the top mural with, I proceed to blast out the skull trio with the airbrush.

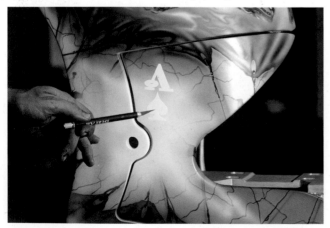

Using my plotter, I create any of my hard edges and apply the template to the white pearl base, the example seen here is the ace of spades.

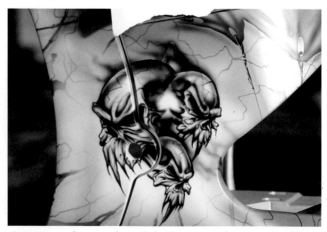

Be sure to have a lot of darks around your template areas to make sure they show up. As I suggested in an earlier step, without these darks the templates would be lost.

Time now to remove the template vinyl. Here you can see the contrast discussed earlier in the shape of the ace and the spade shape.

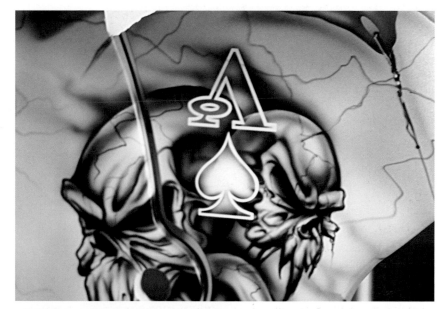

Next, I add highlights and reflection to suggest chrome. These effects are rendered freehand, but really do a great deal to really fatten up the overall look.

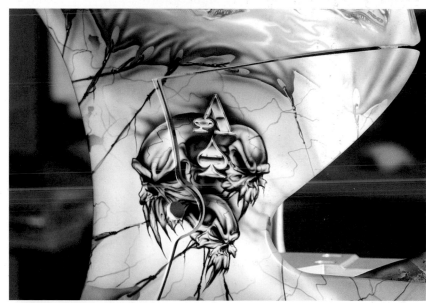

A nice light wash of purple and blue will marry it to the rest of the bike. I continue on the cracking and sewing of the parchment element, as well as finishing all the other images on the scooter. When I'm happy, it's off to the paint booth for 8-10 coats of clear, and then wet sand and polish.

Chapter Six

Dead Girl Walking

Beauty from the Other Side

This project forced me to work on a canvas much different than that provided by most custom bikes. Instead of spending tons of money on elaborate custom sheet metal, the client wanted to put a substantial amount of money straight into his paint job. So instead of having a large custom molded bike as a canvas, I'm challenged to lay out a lot of content on two relatively small surfaces, the gas tank and front fender. The subject matter is figures that are half dead and half alive, as well as the destruction of a modern city. chaos, and a demented version of the client's dog, T- Bone.

Out of the mist approaches a figure. The silhouette of a comely lass, yet something is amiss. As the female figure and dog approach, you realize it's far too late for introductions. Meanwhile the city is in chaos from her passing. On the other side of the metropolis the dark sister revels in deviant pleasure provided by the surrounding morbid creations of her fair haired sister and the city's occupants.

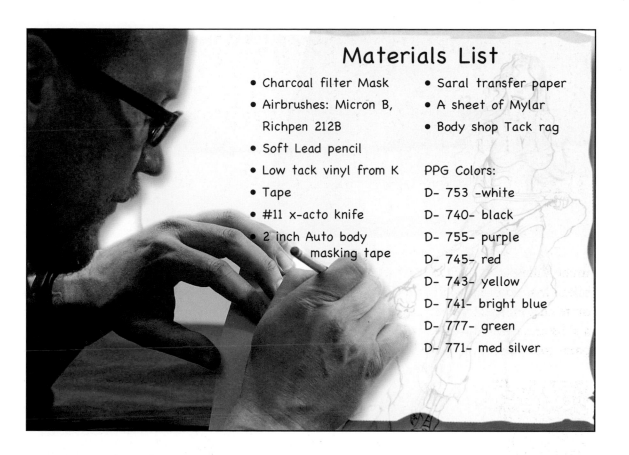

Materials List

- Charcoal filter Mask
- Airbrushes: Micron B, Richpen 212B
- Soft Lead pencil
- Low tack vinyl from K
- Tape
- #11 x-acto knife
- 2 inch Auto body masking tape
- Saral transfer paper
- A sheet of Mylar
- Body shop Tack rag

PPG Colors:

D- 753 -white
D- 740- black
D- 755- purple
D- 745- red
D- 743- yellow
D- 741- bright blue
D- 777- green
D- 771- med silver

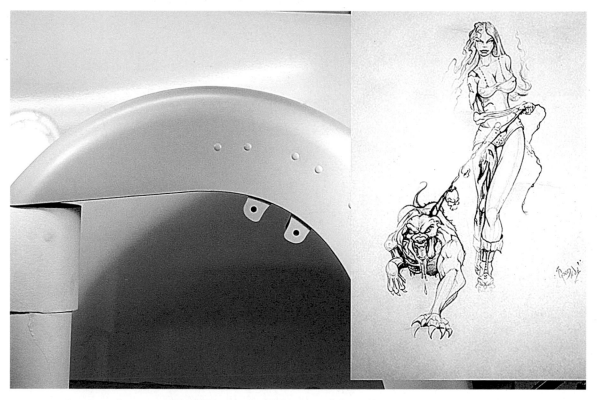

Because there's a shortage of half-living, half-dead models willing to pose, I worked up a couple of sketches in pencil, with a separate color strategy. I sprayed the parts with a warm neutral gray (90% white with 5% black and 5% transparent red). This is the middle of the values I want to end up with when I'm finished.

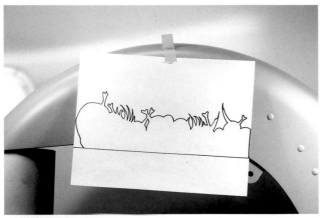

I then draw the outside silhouette of my skull piles. I want to mask this off so I create a contrast between the lighted skull against the darker mid-ground.

I then spray a medium gold color (75% silver 10% trans yellow and 15% trans red) to match the paint on the other existing stock parts. Then darken it in a gradient towards the skull pile.

Using low tack vinyl from K-tape I transfer my skull piles' outside edges to create a mask. I use tape to cover any holes that over spray could leak through.

I further deepen the contrast with a dark purple red color (75% trans red and 25% purple), I want to skull pile to really jump at you when I pull the mask.

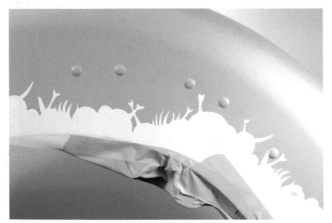

A closer look at the negative mask system just to make sure it's burnished (rubbed down) well to avoid blow throughs.

Now with the mask removed I have a great stark contrast on which to build my skull pile. The warm neutral color we applied in the beginning is in the same family as the rest of the fender.

With a soft-weight lead pencil I start sketching the interplay of skulls and bones. I have to be conscious of how they relate to the outside silhouette of the bone piles.

So with a purple red mixture (about 25% purple and 75% red) I work the little skulls inch by inch. Adding different expressions. No two skulls are the same. The coin I am holding gives you an idea of their actual size.

I keep working the area in the same manner, being sure that the skulls remain fairly horizontal, unless they happen to be rolling down the back of the fender.

Here I am at one with my airbrush approaching the bottom of the fender. For this job I'm using my Micron C airbrush.

A little mist of white never hurts, it helps give a feeling of perspective and eeriness.

As we get to the bottom I want to add depth to the make-shift bone yard, so I am sure to place some fairly large skulls in the foreground.

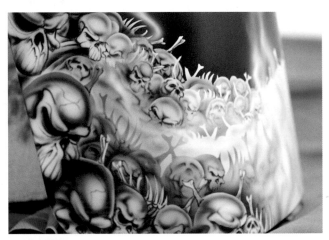

I also paint the skulls in the background with less intensity which also helps to push them to the back.

I then make them progressively smaller toward the background, creating depth and distance in comparison to the foreground skulls.

Here is a view of this side of the fender when completed. The skull piles will provide a sort of frame for the rest of the art to come.

I carry on and finish the opposite side of the fender in the same manner. Every skull is done individually, and each one has a different flavor so to speak. There are close to 300 on this one piece alone.

Time to add the final focal point, which is the image of our ghoul friend and her dog. I lay down some white tinted slightly with purple. It's almost unnoticeable but I like the idea of a little purple in the background. This process is like painting a canvas behind the image, and gives me freedom to lay down darks or pull light from my background.

Using transfer paper I position my original sketch and lightly trace out my most basic shapes for reference. In this case I'm using saral paper, you simply place it under your sketch and it leaves a nice impression you can follow.

Using a photo copy of my original to make a mask, I take the template and block out my dark areas of which I'll play up later to push the figure ahead. The template totally speeds up this process in the early stages.

By spraying my dark shades behind the figure, it gives me a nice shape that I can fill out with my flesh tones to create the figure itself.

I begin to define the shapes of the body (using 75% yellow and 20% red plus 5% blue) using free hand templates I've made from "miler" (clear solvent resistant ridged plastic, the same stuff you print transparencies on) wherever I need a hard edge.

I continue to work the figure's flesh tones, keeping in mind the overall feel of the piece. I don't want the tones of the flesh too wholesome and bright.

For clothing I use a mixture of red and white to create a pink color, and give her a see-through garment.

Now for the dog creature. Using the silhouette I created earlier, I sketch in light pencil lines which will act as a guide.

Using a black-purple mixture I work with the hair and her boney arm. I also increase the intensity of the darks in the background of the figure.

Using the same color as the hair, I add a set of boots and the leash, that's to restrain her dog thing.

I go ahead and blast out the half living mutt using purple with a little red in my airbrush. I keep my detail and lines super tight.

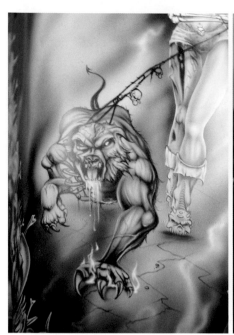  

I add more of a blue-purple feel to the hound and the area surrounding him, I think it is a nice compliment to the warmer yellow-orange of the zombie babe.

Here is a shot of the couple completed for this section. In the space on her left I will add a stone pillar that recedes into the sky.

On the back of the fender I created the second figure using the same procedures, having her appear out of the bone yard holding a trophy.

I want to establish a mid ground to work the foreground and distance against. A stone pillar will be the ideal starting point. Here you see how I've taped it off with body shop masking tape.

After making sure I protect the background, and the rest of my piece, from overspray I manipulate the area to appear cylindrical and add textures to suggest stone. I could go into great detail on each phase of this, but really it is open to your interpretation.

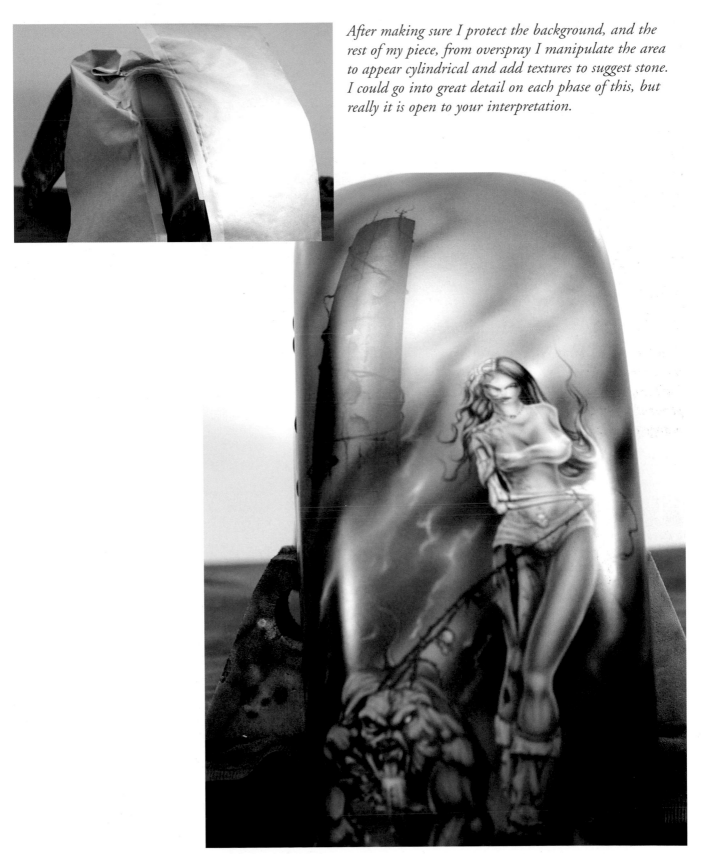

With the main ideas complete, I'm free to roam about the fender adding disturbing images and curious details.

Chapter Seven

Dirt Merchant

Stars and More Stars

This Bike is awesome! Take a modern day four-stroke MX race bike, tear it apart and turn it into an old school track race bike. The thinking on this is way outside the box and I really enjoyed being involved in this project.

The idea is to give this old school race bike a modern MX race bike style paint job with a menacing feel to it. We started this job, as we often do, by stripping the parts to bare steel and aluminum.

Here is the "Dirt Merchant" on Sauble Beach, located in Ontario. We needed a nice location to shoot the final pictures and with the blue sky reflecting off the water it was a beautiful accent to this unique project.

Materials

- Plotter & interface
- Corel Draw
- PPG's – White basecoat, pearl white, orange pearl, Chrome yellow
- Black, Trans. Red. Silver Metallic
- Low Tack Vinyl
- Red Stripping Enamel
- DTM Primer
- Body Filler
- Rich Pen C series – Suction
- Jeweler's files

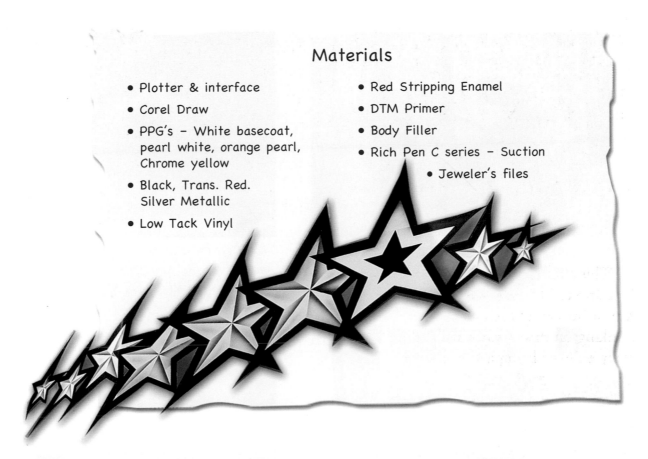

Here is a shot of the major components mocked up before they come into my shop - minus, the one-off front end that is being manufactured as I work on the rest of the parts.

I remove any lumps or welding slag from the modified areas on the stock frame as well from the new fabbed parts.

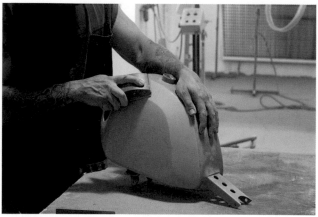

Next I get the sheet metal straight. I will pressure test and seal the fuel tank. After body work, I shoot it with 5 coats of PPG's DTM primer. After it cures, I block everything flat with 180 grit paper.

The larger components go off to the sandblaster: for clean up, and to promote adhesion of the filler material. The more delicate parts I do myself in our blasting cabinet, especially aluminum parts.

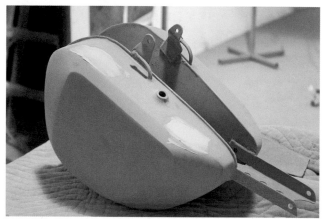

Sometimes you will find low spots after shooting the preliminary primer. I address these by using a light weight polyester putty, then block them out with 180 grit before our secondary primer coats.

Using a jeweler's file, I make sure all the edges are clean on the detail areas of the sheet metal. I don't really want to put a lot of polyester filler on the Aluminum side covers, just minimal amounts.

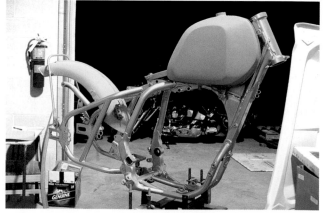

After another 3 coats of DTM primer, I final sand all the parts with 600-800 wet paper. Here I carefully place the prepped stage sheet metal on the painted frame to get a feel for my blank canvas.

Tom and I came up with a general theme for the bike using pencils and markers. I then transfer my ideas to Corel Draw, the drawings can be used to tell my plotter (vinyl cutter) what to do.

After considering the most efficient way to lay down color sequences, I choose to spray everything in a fine white pearl basecoat, then add 2 coats of intercoat clear (D- 895) and let dry for 1 hour.

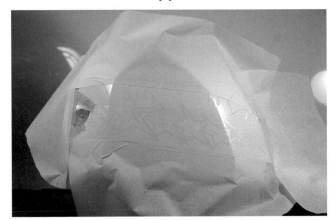

I use my vector file to cut out a template of my first element, the 3 dimensional star field. I remove the areas I'm about to spray, and mask beyond my target area to avoid overspray on my white background.

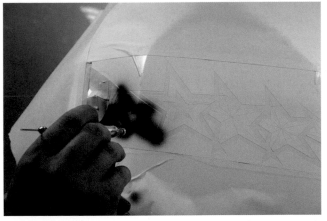

The next step is to spray my borders with straight black base in my airbrush. Be sure to get an even coverage, but not to build up huge edges by spraying tons of material.

I pick a light source and start to add dark reflections to the show side of our 3-D stars. It's kind of an alternating pattern.

The main idea is to juxtaposition light and dark, if you have a dark edge on one side leave its counter part light.

I remove the other side of the bevel on the star and suggest subtle reflections… using the same black color.

I continue with the rest of the stars in sequence, using the same concept positioning dark against light in the beveled areas of the stars

Here are the stars complete to this stage. With all the masking on, you have to rely on your master plan and original vision to understand the look your trying to achieve in the end.

Remove the rest of the vinyl mask you applied earlier. Be sure not to muck up the pearl white underneath. For this reason I keep my hands clean throughout the painting process.

Star graphic element exposed. Here I can see the width of my dark black boarders which will contrast against the yellow orange fade that is coming next.

Next, I place a mask over the graphic, leaving only the background exposed. I shift the mask 1/10 of an inch to top left, this will give me a fine white pearl highlight afterward on the outside black border. Then back to the booth, where I lay down a nice coat of yellow pearl over the entire tank.

I then cut out 600 stars on my plotter. I use only the outside contours of the stars and skew them to indicate motion. I place them on the sheet metal wherever they look cool.

I apply the stars en mass. There are over 300 on the tank alone ranging from 1/8 to 4 inches, and as I go you will see some patterns emerge.

With the stars in place where I feel they will make the most impact, you will notice they're placed over the original yellow pearl basecoat that we had sprayed earlier. My plan is to create a fade from light orange to deep orange, almost red, towards the bottom of the tank. Then a light mist of straight yellow pearl over the top of the tank.

Back to the spray booth, and I drop a 4 color fade from top to bottom of the tank (yellow, orange, pink and, red). Then apply a light coat of yellow pearl over the top of the tank again.

Now to the task of removing the star templates....So if everything goes as planned, I should have nice yellow pearl stars with sharper contrast in the red areas, and diminishing contrast in the top yellow areas.

300 stars, and four and a half hours later, I lay a drop shadow under the stars using trans/red. Then I clean up any blow outs and sharpen any fuzzy areas.

I remove the initial mask that covers the 3 dimensional stars. POW! The black really rocks against the orange basecoat below.

"Here they are with all the vinyl taken off and the edges tacked to remove any loose millage that may have built up in the yellow-orange spraying process".

To add character and personality to some of the stars, I use masking tape and spray black to give the 3 dimensional stars a more hooked and menacing feel, again, suggesting forward motion.

I do the same thing with the bottom edge of the stars. I find that with the plotter sometimes it is difficult to create the curving edges around the contours, in this case the black sharp borders of the stars, so I resort to body tape and meticulous masking each section piece by piece.

Shot of the finished black border work and the 3 dimensional stars. Giving the ole school racing look, with a newer modern feel. Yamaha was the sponsor for this gig and since their corporate colors have switched to yellow, black and white this year (2005), I think it is bang on.

The last element in this graphic is old-school silver leaf for the star. I place vinyl mask to contain my sizing for the silver leaf. I could brush it free hand, but I really want sharp edges. In this case I am using a quick size which sets up in approximately 1 hour.

I apply a thin layer of size with a fine sable brush. Sizing is like a glue basically, it's composed of the same elements as shellac. Try not to overdue it, applying a thin film will suffice.

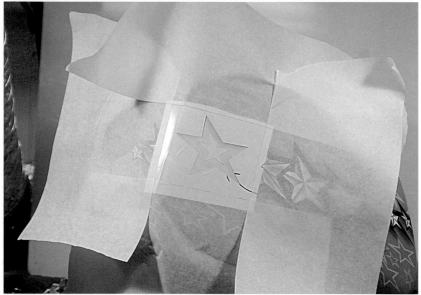

I mask off the surrounding area to protect the fresh base coats from the leafing process. Sometimes a stray piece of leaf can adhere to the base coat, especially if the base coat is fresh.

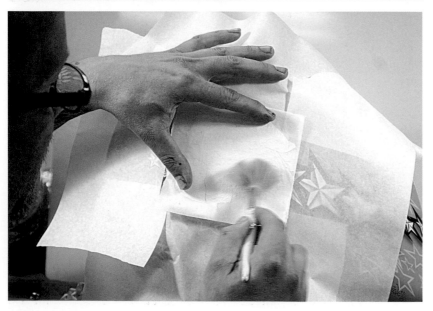

I carefully lay down the silver leaf over the size. Normally I would remove the template, but since we are against the clock on this one I'm concerned that the leaf might adhere to the fresh basecoats, which I would normally allow to dry for 24 hours. After letting the sizing tack approximately 45 minutes, you will know when it is ready if you touch it with your knuckle and it feels similar to rubbing it on glass. Not sticky, but you will feel friction.

Using a woman's make-up brush, I gently remove the excess leaf from the sheet I have applied. It is a good idea to put some plastic underneath you because leaf gets everywhere, especially if there is a breeze it will be in every corner of your shop.

Here's my silver leaf with all the excess cleaned off, be sure to vacuum the area of any leaf that may be lying around or it will only cause you problems later.

Carefully remove your mask, take your time and you should have a nice clean edge around your silver leaf. Normally I would allow it a couple of days to dry. When I do clear coat it I use a medium dry coat and let it sit for 10 -15 minutes before adding the other clearcoats.

Chapter Eight

Eagle Fairing

A Prey's Eye View

In this project, the client saw a canvas I did with an eagle on it. That original image started as a photograph which I interpreted in painting the canvas. For the fairing image I started by taking photos of that canvas, including close ups and detail pictures. The photos became my reference point. The trick in this case is to take an existing image I've already done on a flat surface, and recreate it on a piece of three dimensional fiberglass, the motorcycle fairing.

The image before clear coat, notice there is only a suggestion of the wings against a night sky. The subtle shadows in transparent color will be applied in the sun, but not draw your eye from the central details

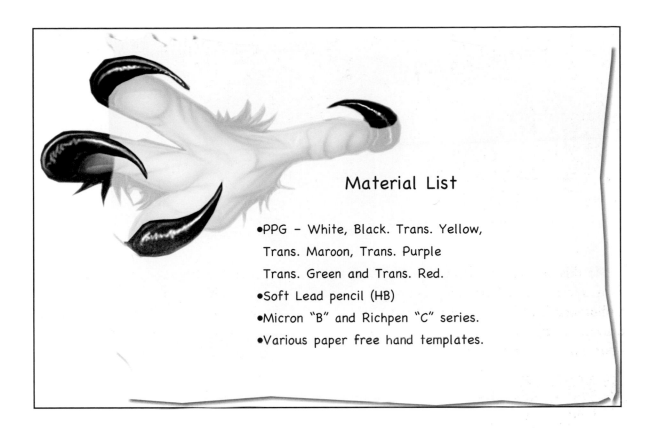

Material List

• PPG – White, Black. Trans. Yellow, Trans. Maroon, Trans. Purple Trans. Green and Trans. Red.
• Soft Lead pencil (HB)
• Micron "B" and Richpen "C" series.
• Various paper free hand templates.

The first stage is to strip the fairing, re-prime it and sand. The last step in the preparation is 600 grit wet. Next, I apply 3 coats of black basecoat, which will be the foundation of the art-work that follows.

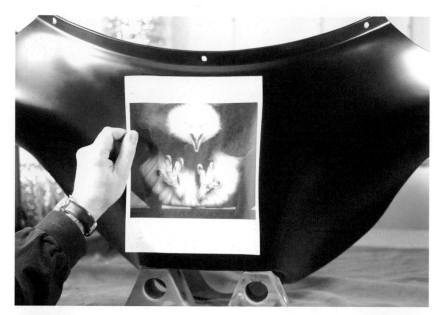

Here I size up the original image, the reference that I mentioned earlier. This is my interpretation of an eagle ready to attack, perhaps coming at you if you were its prey. Call it a prey's eye view.

A close up of my reference. I like to keep it black and white. All I'm concerned about is the light and dark values.

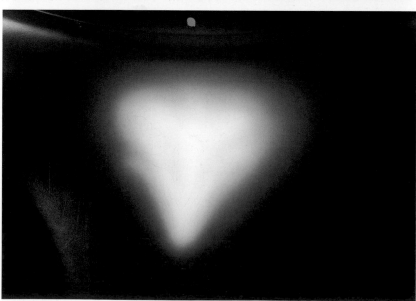

In the next step I want to create a white atmosphere, so I reverse paint onto the black with white basecoat. This gives me a starting point. When I did the canvas it was a white canvas, and I worked everything back from there. This time I am doing the opposite. I have to build up the white and then build the transparent tones on top of that.

Once I have a general shape of the area that I want to lighten up, I go in with a soft lead pencil. I very, very lightly (stress lightly) block out the main composition of the face of the eagle. I don't try and get into too much detail here because I don't want to marry myself to all those little lines. I will let the airbrush do the details as I go.

Next, using a mix (transparent yellow, transparent maroon and a couple drops of purple) I start building up flesh tones in the beak and mouth areas. The eyes are going to be kind of a fleshy color. I very gently build it up, then I will knock it back with darker colors later. You don't want to over work the image at this stage.

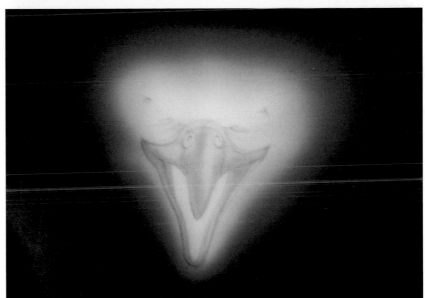

Darkening my original mixture I add a little bit of purple, and another drop of red, then go back in and start deepening the shadows and richening up these areas, pushing them back.

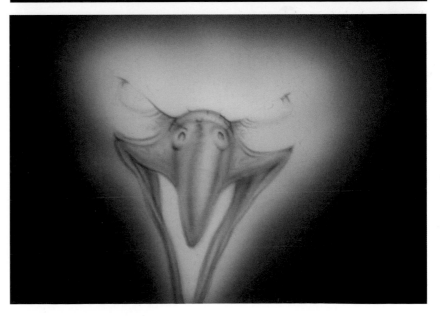

The next step is to start feeding the darker areas, the darker shadows, with color. I use a little bit more purple and a couple drops of green, this gives me a very dark color, but not a real black. Over and over again I say, "black over powers everything." This color is a nice dark shade, but it also has components that complement the colors that are in the painting already.

I've added some transparent red colors to the tongue and inner mouth areas, and a hint in the eyes, maybe. No one has white eyes. Plus, even eagles can be slightly sinister.

At this point, I start feeding some of the black background back, to reduce the white around the face area that seems excessive. Also, I need some dark to extend the outer feather areas.

74

I have added a few white highlights to the face which makes the tongue look wet and more convincing. I'm also just starting to work the lower feather areas.

Here you can see I have been developing some of the feathers with the use of free hand techniques, and some templates that I cut out of paper. This gives it a buried look, some hard edges and some soft edges.

Here are the face feathers, complete thus far. I constantly try to get the direction of the art to flow with the shape of the fairing.

In the same way that I've developed the colors in the beak, I move on to the talons. The procedure used for the talons is similar to that used for the beak but not identical.

With the talons complete in their dark tones, I move to the tail feathers. Here I suggest details, using the darkest of the mixtures that I used in the talons.

I apply white in general shapes where I want to punch out the black background. I use this procedure often, you always need a light color upon which to build transparent colors and details in the foreground.

Next I add some cool colors, namely transparent purple and blues, to push the warm colors of the feet forward and the tail portion into the background atmosphere suggesting depth.

I develop the claw and talon structure, working from light tones to dark, keeping in mind I want these shapes way in front of the back tail feathers, which appear to recede into cooler color values.

I add white behind the wings to indicate their shape, then I add nice complementary colors that go with the bike. All that's left are highlights in the talons and facial area to give life to our attacking eagle.

I tend to concentrate on the central portion of my design to give a sense of closeness to the details. Less effort in the outer fringes helps lock your eye to the center. It works very well on objects that are large, by not covering them entirely you can maintain a deep color on the outside, not making the bike too over run with bright colors in the top portions. The purple and oranges work well to complement each other.

Chapter Nine

Leering Skull

A Truly Evil Smile

This NASCAR helmet will be victim to my creative desires because, as the client said, "I don't care just do your thing." So I have an opportunity to show you three elements I have in my mind. A freehand skull, some chrome graphics, and realistic or interruptive fire. So here we go.

A look at the top portion of the helmet during the airbrush phase. I'm keeping my lines large and aggressive for better visibility from a distance.

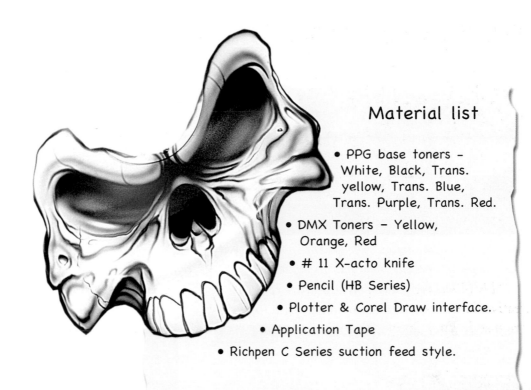

Material list

- PPG base toners – White, Black, Trans. yellow, Trans. Blue, Trans. Purple, Trans. Red.
- DMX Toners – Yellow, Orange, Red
- # 11 X-acto knife
- Pencil (HB Series)
- Plotter & Corel Draw interface.
- Application Tape
- Richpen C Series suction feed style.

I begin by base-coating the helmet with pure white because it's more efficient to reverse tape the graphic portion. What I mean by this is that if I were to spray the helmet black and spray in the graphic white, it would mean a lot more work to avoid overspray, and in the end I would use a lot more masking material.

Next, I design some tribal style graphics on my Corel draw program, and cut them out on my plotter. Because the backing paper and the vinyl are both white, it's a little hard to see the design.

I apply the masking system using application tape, basically wide clear adhesive tape, that keeps every thing together during the transfer to the helmet.

Here is a closeup of the tribal flames applied to the helmet, I'm checking to be sure everything is pressed down to the surface to avoid any bleeds or blow thru.

Once I'm satisfied with the symmetry I move to my booth and apply black basecoat. I do not hog on the paint. My masking is still in place for the chrome flames. I leave the top of the helmet white for now.

I start the interpretive flames using straight white, and emulate the twisting and turning images I see when I look at fire, just keep everything moving in the same direction.

Next, I nail the whole shebang with trans yellow (DMX yellow tinted with 3 parts 895 and reduced 2:1 with medium reducer).

I then go in with DMX orange, reduced and concocted like the previous yellow, but I only hit the outside edges of the shape indicating a cooler temperature.

I do the same with a DMX red mixture, except I'm only hitting the extreme edges of the flame. This red over the outside orange really pushes this shape into the cooler background

I go back in with the white and rework my hot areas, which are the central portions of the flames. This helps to add some interesting dynamics.

I nail it again with trans yellow like I did earlier using the same mixture. I mist the fire area with the DMX yellow again to blend it all together. I keep up the process of heating up and knocking back until I'm satisfied.

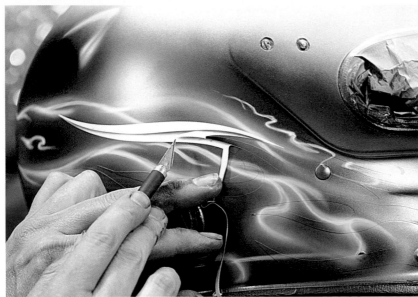

Next, it's time to chrome up the tribal flame graphics. Using an extremely sharp x-acto knife I cut out the bottom of my imaginary horizon line in the graphic. I use a weak black and hit the bottom, creating a tight fade.

I carry on, section by section of the chrome flame, indicating reflections of the sky and horizon. Be careful not to get too dark overall.

I then enhance the sky effect on the top reflections of our chrome flame. Don't let the blue get down into the white transitions of your horizon line.

Then I switch to a brown mixture (25% trans red 70% trans yellow 5% purple) and hit the bottom of the horizon line. I return to the white and add some "chingg" to suggest high lights, and indicate the interplay of the flames with the chrome.

I move to the top of the helmet. The goal is to put a leering skull on top, so I get out my pencil and lightly block out my idea.

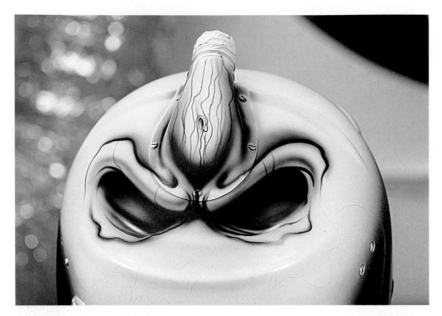

Using a blackish purple mixture (80% black 17% purple 3 % red), I start beating out the features of our angry friend. I start with the eyes and brow.

The face begins to emerge. I just keep pushing the darks back and the lights forward.

Using transparent purple I start to smooth out my transition areas within the skull, creating a nice vibrant color.

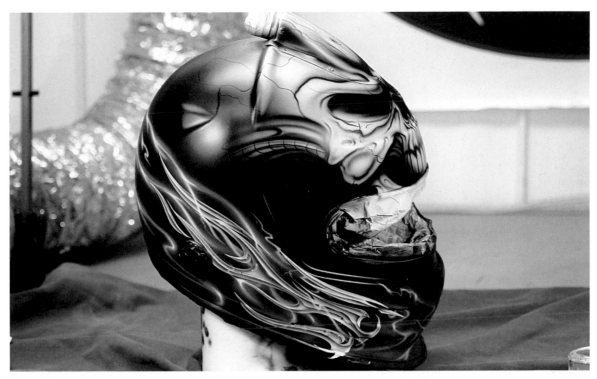

I use the same purple to marry my dark areas to the top portion of the helmet. It works great against the orange yellows.

A little straight white, and some eye candy, and we are done and ready for clear coat. For the eyes I use a circle template to keep them nice and tight.

Chapter Ten

Kiss Tribute Hood

French Kiss on a German Car

In this project I was asked to create a version of an album cover from the heavy metal era. It turned out to be a blast from my past. Bobby Hooper, the man who commissioned the piece was totally amped. With the combined energy of two Kiss fans, and an understanding that I could use artistic license in the recreation, I jumped into the Kiss Tribute. When the project was all done, Bobby enjoyed it so much he wanted me to do more of the car, which you will see in the next chapter. First though, let's look at the this first project, which started with the hood.

Here Bobby and I are the day he picked up the vehicle.

Materials List:

- Charcoal filter mask
- Airbrushes: Micron B and Richpen 212B
- Opaque projector
- Light pencil
- Body shop masking tape 3/4 & 2inch
- Plastic or paper for overspray
- Body shop tack rag

- PPG colors:
D- 753 –white	D- 755 – purple
D- 745 – red	D- 743 – yellow
D- 777 – green	D- 740 – black

I paint the hood white basecoat to start, because that is what I see a majority of, and I can always feed the black back in to match the car's color.

Next I transfer the image with help from an opaque projector. I keep it light as this is a guide for size more than anything.

I use the same principles and color sequence to create the women in the center. They slowly become more eerie from left to right.

I begin with the women using a blackish color (I mix up red, purple and green until I get a deep blackish color). I used this same color throughout the image, changing features and attitudes as I go.

Here you see the gals fully transformed into complete demons not ashamed of their thirst for blood. Quite a contrast from their sisters on the left side of the hood.

Next, I add flesh tones with trans yellow and various mixes of trans red. A couple of drops of purple are good to calm it down. I add reds and blue to cool shadows in the faces and some of the mist.

Here is the whole complete gaggle of ghouls. Now I start tying in my darks to the bottom of the hood.

Once I've completed the faces, it gives me a feeling of confidence as I progress to the next stage.

Using the same dark color I mixed for the girls, I work off my reference picture and complete Gene. Gotta love those boots.

Time to work on the bodies, being sure to capture the nuances of the costumes and personalities.

Here's a look at the completed figures, notice how I left the areas of mist light between Paul Stanley and Ace. No sense filling in detail here only to cover it later.

A close up of the lads in their full contact rock 'n roll gear. The subtle tones in their shirts and leathers will play off the background nicely.

I remask my pillars to protect them from the onslaught of the background application. I also create an arch way over the top of our heroes.

I need to create a cool set of marble pillars, so I mask off the shapes which helps avoid overspray on my background and also gives me a nice crisp edge.

Using a large spray gun, I feed the black base of the rest of the car into the background, leaving white areas for my complimentary colors and the mist.

I remove the mask system. You can see that I've used a combo of yellows and blues to create the pillars. I used dark purple to create the shadow at the top and left the bottom white for the mist.

Removing my masks, I balance all my colors with trans blue, green, pearl purple and just a tinge of red.

Using white in the airbrush I enhance the mist and look for ways to add drama to the overall composition.

Here is the team complete with highlights and details, looking ghoulishly good. Check out the hint of deep red top left behind the pillar, a nice compliment to all the blue aquas.

Here's the car, cleared, assembled and ready to roll, or should I say, rock 'n roll.

Chapter Eleven

Hot Rod Punch Buggy

When One is Not Enough

Two years ago I painted a Kiss tribute on the hood of this Volkswagen. The owner, Bobby Hooper, or Hoop as we call him admits that the art on the car, "is like a tattoo, they are addicting". So he came back for more, but not necessarily the same. The idea this time is to create a gothic work-out club. Bobby, you see, owns a fitness club and decided to incorporate that idea as well as the name "Sportsmakers" into the design. So here we go into round two, let's see what emerges when we combine Bobby's ideas with my own twisted interpretation and creative abilities.

Here is a shot of the VW, complete with its new artwork, clear-coated and assembled.

Material list

- PPG's – Black, purple, White, Trans. Red, Trans. blue, Trans. Yellow
- PPG's – Global D- 8753 Sealer
- PPG's – DX 330 wax and grease remover
- Plotter & interface
- Tack Rag
- Scotchbrite Pad (equivalent to 600 wet)
- Body shop 2" tape
- Paper
- HB Pencil

After moving all the bike parts out of the way we get our next victim into the booth, where it will live until I'm done.

First came the bath, then I begin taping up the bug. Don't forget the trunk and door jams, overspray can creep in there and ruin the job.

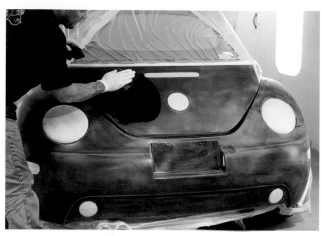

Next comes the wipe down with wax and grease remover (one that leaves no residue behind).

This step is crucial, be sure to protect areas not being worked on from overspray, the paint mist that lands on the already-finished parts. To remove it can sometimes be very time consuming.

Next I begin by spraying 3 medium coats of PPG's D – 8753. This aids in adhesion, as well as leveling scratches left by the Scotchbrite. I also find it helps to eliminate any static on the plastic parts.

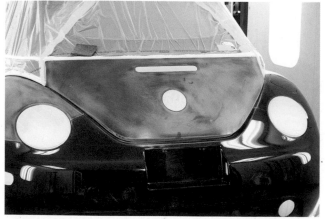

Using a grey Scotchbrite pad (equivalent of 600 grit paper) I rough up the original paint. I work each panel methodically, being careful not to miss any edges or grooves.

I've come up with a couple of really quick structural compositions to begin my first image. I keep the sketches light and mainly think about proportions rather than detail.

I now decide on the color palette in which I'm going to work. For the back of the vehicle I want to create a particularly hellish feel so my dominate hue will be warm reds and oranges. Then I want to fade around the sides with darker purples and burgundies. If you don't have one, be sure to invest in an analogous color wheel, it helps you picture your color strategy.

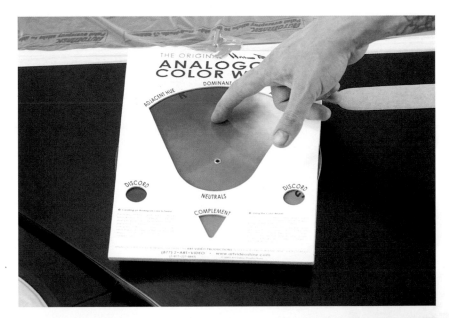

Here I want to establish the basic form while keeping my background dark. I cut out a template of my drawing from paper and use repositioning spray adhesive. I lightly spray white to step away from the black background.

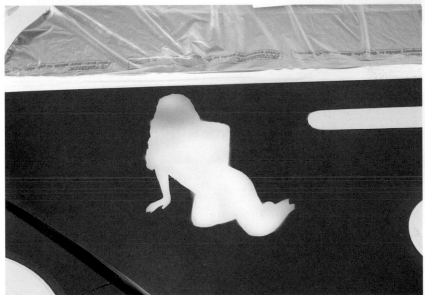

Using a black basecoat, one that is equal to the car's original color, I knock back the areas I want to disappear in shadow, or fade off into the background color. This is one time I do use true black for obvious reasons.

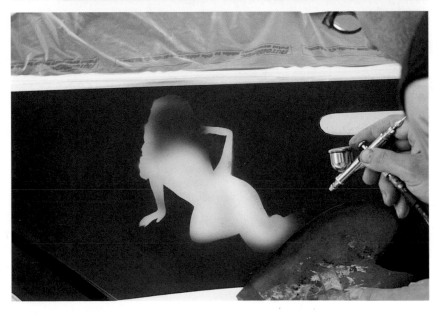

Over to the mixing bank where I keep all my toners, I mix a blend of trans red, trans yellow, and a little purple to establish my control color. This is the color which all the other colors on my pallet will revolve around, and the color I use for most of my shadows and shaping of contours.

After lightly sketching in my basic form, I use my control color and soften the edges as well as push back the bulk of my dark areas. I sometimes employ the use of a free hand shield to get some of my crisp edges.

Using white, and switching back and forth to my control color, I free hand in the main dark and light contrast areas beginning to add form to my figure. I keep working with my control color until I'm satisfied I can't get my darks any darker without over working them.

Since we are going way out of the realm of reality on this piece, I've decided to have our girl lounging in a small lava flow. I use straight white and really build my hot spots. After a light wash of trans yellow (a soft mist of the color from my airbrush) over the figure, I continue working my control color.

I add a few drops of purple and increase the depth of my shadow areas. With some white in my airbrush I rework the hair, add a whip and suggest a subtle sort of face. I want it to remain mostly in shadow for her glowing eyes, which I will add later. A little more trans yellow in her hair and I move on.

By using 2 inch body shop tape I mask off my pillars in the background. By adding light behind these forms I can quickly create cylinder like objects (pillars) and embellish them to fit my ideas at the time.

I really keep my eye on the direction in which the lava moves. I think about the effect gravity has on a liquid, and how to obtain the best perspective as the lava flows toward the viewer.

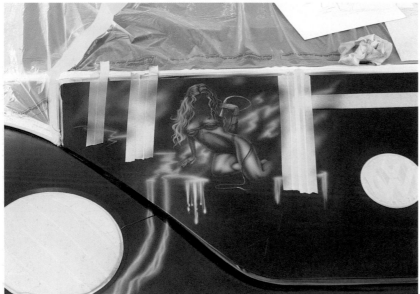

Using trans yellow I spray over the white lava lightly, then use trans red and spray over the outer edges to make them an orange hue.

Then I go back in with straight white to emphasize the hot centers, again making a nice crisp contrast against the under-painting we did earlier on the lava.

None of this happens fast. Now I do another light wash of trans yellow which really melts everything back together, giving the illusion or appearance of radiant heat rising from the lava.

Using white and dark purple, I suggest a foreground or rock precipice, and stairway. I then begin a fire storm, starting up the center in the same manner that I used to create the lava, but this time I want the white under painting to mimic movement upward.

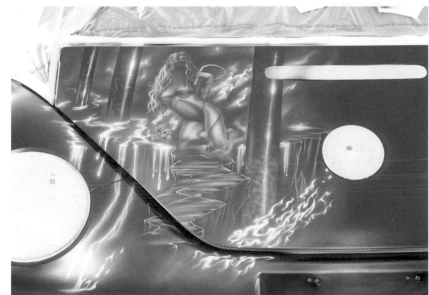

Now to the vinyl cutter (plotter) where I design the client's company name in a Goth-style lettering. I apply the vinyl letters to create a mask which will protect the black background while I paint the firestorm. Once I'm done, I remove the vinyl letters and symbol, leaving a nice black logo with crisp edges (this is also known as reverse taping).

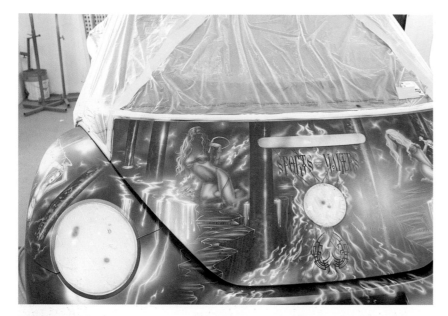

This is a look at the left quadrant of the project with the artwork phase complete.

Detail shot shows the passenger side rear fender. You can really see how I used dramatic lighting here.

The drivers' side rear fender area complete. The texture in the pillars was accomplished by using free hand templates that I made from paper.

This image is representative of a bizarre treadmill in the gym, one which you can never leave.

Bobby and I with a finished Bug, just in time for spring touring.

Chapter Twelve

Devil's Playground

Machines with Heart

For this project I flew to Idaho where my friend, and client, Steve lives. I left home with nothing more than a pencil, which was promptly confiscated at customs. With no computer, vinyl cutter or other luxuries, I proceeded to embark on an adventure of hunter-gatherer. Securing equipment and product indigenous to the area became my first task. Next came the sketches and layouts of the complex graphics that would cover Steve's Big Truck from one end to the other.

Here's a finished shot of the driver's side door with our boney gleeful jockey riding his hellish creation. The piece is approximately ten feet long, and I think it should make a great visual statement just sitting at a stop light.

Materials List

- PPG's – Black, Purple pearl,
- Trans. Red, Trans. Blue,
- Trans. Green
- PPG's – DMX – Yellow, Orange,
- Red.Lead Pencil (HB)

- Richpen C series – suction feed
- Large format spray guns
- Charcoal mask
- Application Tape
- # 11 X –acto knife

Say hello to my little friend. This is how the vehicle came to me, ready to paint thanks to Todd and his buds. At first the square footage of the project overwhelmed me, but I got over it. I start with the preliminary sketches and layouts, keeping them loose and basic as usual.

I start by taping the door jams and fender wells to avoid creeping overspray that could enter the clean black interior.

...be sure to use new blades and just cut the tape. The sharp blades give you more control.

Next, I lay down application tape, being sure to remove any loose spots or bubbles with a squeegee. Now I sketch my first element on the truck.

Here is a close up of the cut-out application tape and masking, this will give us a nice crisp edge to work off of later.

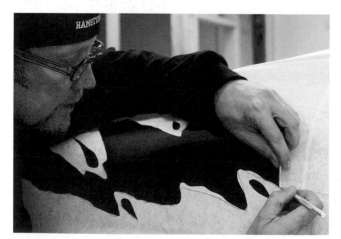

With a # 11 x-acto knife I carefully cut out the areas to be exposed. Don't hulk out and cut deep...

Using 24 inch body shop paper, I mask the outside edges to avoid overspray. Don't under estimate the creeping ability of overspray.

In this step I use bright orange from my mixing bank. It's opaque and builds color without the need for white under painting. Using a French curve ellipse, I proceed to create random background texture to give the impression of depth.

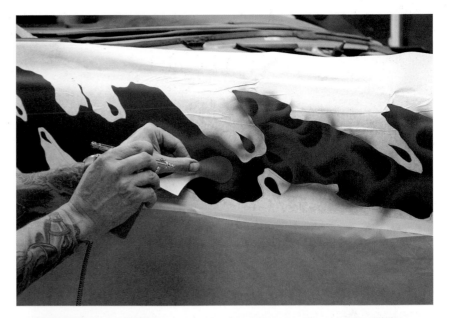

Next, I create a candy mixture using PPG's DMX series. It's a color concentrate that I add to a clear basecoat binder. I then reduce it to a spray-able viscosity of about 2:1. Next, I mist a light coat of this red candy on top of my orange shape, using a detail gun, to knock them back in intensity.

I repeat the process seen at the top of the page with the curve template and the same orange. The orange I applied earlier is darker now due to the candy red topcoat applied in the last step, so this application of orange will be lighter. I'm looking for dark areas, or windows, to fill up with the lighter tone for contrast.

Using opaque yellow I then add light-energy, winding the bright color into the tunnels I've created earlier with my template

Another coat of DMX, but this time I use an orange mixture, reduced exactly like our earlier application of orange.

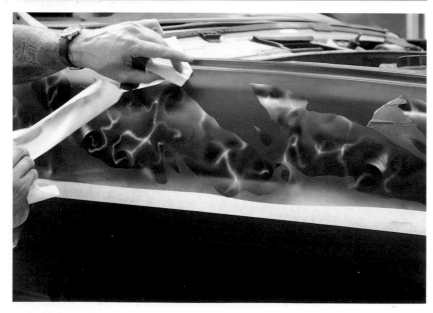

Now I remove the masking system. Always be sure to get any adhesive off the black basecoat by using PPG's DX 320 wipe.

Using pure white basecoat, I then air-brush the outer texture, the stretching sheet metal, bearing in mind a constant light source.

A transparent purple wash over the white I've just sprayed is a good compliment to the reds and oranges within the tear. The purple wash is just trans purple reduced with medium reducer, approximately 2 parts reducer to 1 part paint, sprayed from my airbrush at about 8 inches from the surface. I give all the white a nice even mist coat.

Using pure black I create the stitching that holds the tear together, I seldom use pure black, but in this case I wanted extreme contrast against the graphic. Going back in with white, I pop a few highlights onto the appropriate parts of the ripples in the sheet metal.

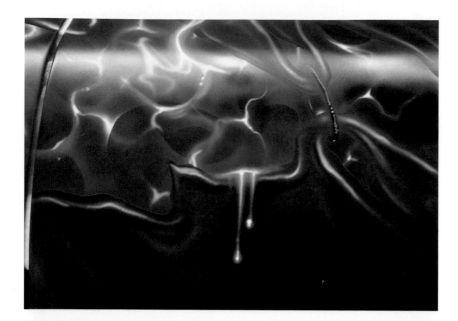

Here is a close up of some of the eye candy, namely the dripping lava and "stitching" that holds the tear together.

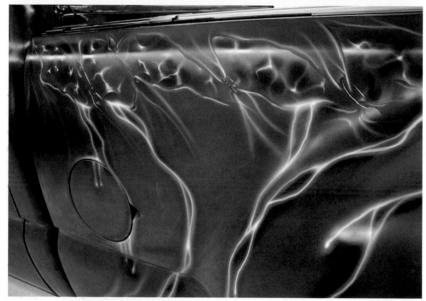

These are the lava flows that run down the quarter panels, I try to follow the contours of the vehicle just like liquid would flow naturally.

I also run the lava down the door pillars to sort of add some light and color to the top of the truck.

For composition sake I want to shoot, or project, my original sketch on the side of the truck in order to get a feel for placement and size. When projecting on black, the light is gobbled up and isn't conducive to a clean reference sketch. So I decide to use 24 inch application tape to mask the vicinity of my first image. This will allow me to better see the projected image (on the white tape), and also control the overspray created by the larger gun and the white basecoat.

I then use a large format spray gun and apply a medium dry coat of white to the area I've exposed in the application tape mask system. Wear your respirator!

Using a light lead pencil (HB) I draw in the major components of my sketch, leaving the fine detail to be created when I'm actually airbrushing. When doing work like this be careful not to contaminate the truck with the oil from your hands during the sketching. You can occasionally clean the areas of contact with DX 320 wipe.

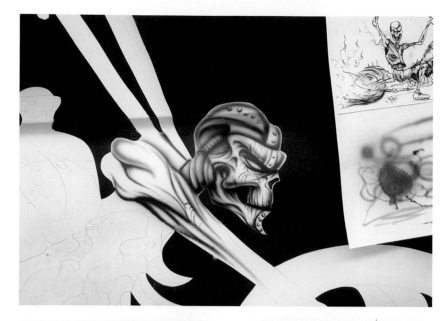

I start cutting out my malevolent friend with a transparent maroon mix (trans red 75%, purple 20% and green 5%). Working off my original design, I begin at the headlight. It seemed like a good place to start to get a feel for the color I chose.

Here I am developing the texture of the sinew that holds the fuel tank. The beauty of not having a ton of reference lines is that you can create on the fly, sort of designing as you go.

Our demonic daredevil emerges complete with fashion-conscious vest. I like the way his high five hand works in front of the other graphic elements.

A progression shot carrying on into the legs. I'm constantly flicking my concentration over the other areas I've worked, making adjustments for balance in the shadow areas.

This shows a progression into the rest of the image. Just remember, be sure to make up enough of your color to last through the whole project. You can remix, but it's a lot easier to roll through the entire painting without running out.

Using white, I under-paint the burnout and the cigar smoke. I then give the "Bike Thing" and the sinewy specter a case of heartburn by adding heat and lava in the key areas.

A close up of his head, the main thing here is to notice the highlight on the right side of the figure, it helps lose the cut out look, or masked white under painting.

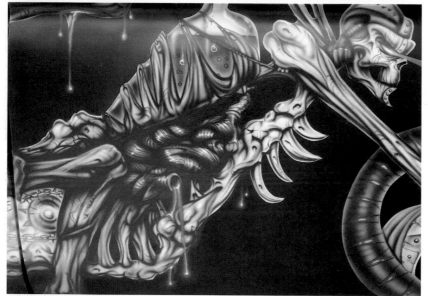

I use the lava to give a little life to the heart of the motor.

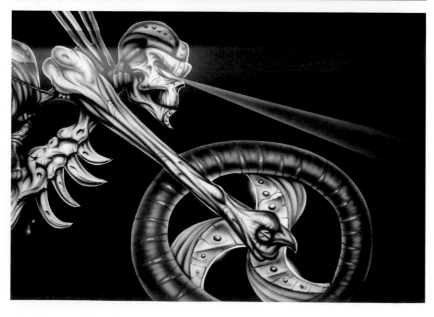

Slashed tires reveal a molten center. Just another point of interest that strays from the norm.

Using white basecoat, I suggest motion in the drive line and the rear tire.

Dark grey is used to indicate the misshapen tire, and the chain, in motion.

I then heat up the burnout using the same principles mentioned at the beginning of the chapter.

Details are extremely important, note the little things like the flying, frying rubber.

Using darks and lights in silhouette, I create a hellish panorama. The strange rock formations contain personal hidden requests by the client.

Hang Ten, a close up of the creatures hand against the torn or ripped graphic.

114

I use a series of loose templates, cut out of Bristol board, to create the mountains in the background and heat, as well as the lava, which forms pools and rivers.

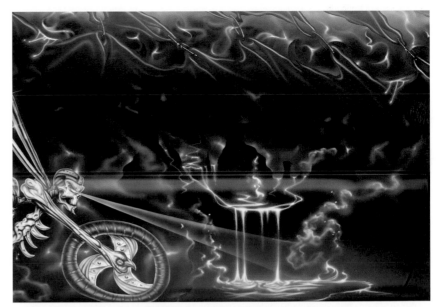

By adding darks against lights, and lights against darks, behind my figure I lose the pasted look.

This is an overall shot of the passenger side. It's a lot of real estate to cover with an airbrush.

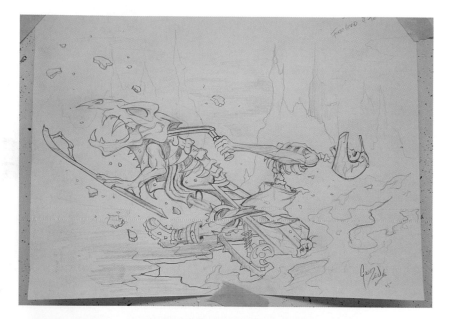

The next sequence reflects the client's fascination with flying up extremely steep mountains at high velocity on snow machines. Generally speaking, the color sequences are similar to the burnout, but with a few twists. So I begin by taping off with application tape.

Using the # 11 x-acto I cut out the outer edge of my design. Just be cautious not to press too hard and damage the underlying basecoat. Sharp blades are a must.

A medium-light basecoat of white will do the trick. I use a large format gun for this process. Be sure to pay attention to safety by wearing your respirator.

I remove the application tape revealing the silhouette of the image. Notice that I've left the back of the sled dark against a light background, this will really help with the illusion of heat later on in the project.

I develop the details in the same manner as the chopper in the previous steps using a mix (75% red 20% purple 5% green).

I continue airbrushing in all the details as I go just letting my imagination run wild.

I add some more elements like guts and flesh to the sled, as well as heat in the exhaust pipes.

Using the transparent colors and sequences for heat seen in the previous segment, I create a wicked rooster tail to suggest horse power and movement.

To emphasize the heat from below, I create a secondary light source from above. I choose purple because it's a perfect compliment to the oranges and reds. To do this I spray a trans purple wash to the top side of my design. I simply reduce trans purple basecoat and spray a light mist coat from about 8-12 inches, watching for even coverage.

Next, I complete the background in the same manner as the other side of the truck with lava flows and strange scenery.

I then go in with white in my airbrush and enhance highlight areas throughout the image.

Next, is a simple matter of adding more eye candy such as lava drips, smoke and all the rest. I'm just kind of rounding everything out.

This is a great view of the driver's door. The look of glee is evident on our boney buddy as he hurtles forward from his fiery platform. Even thought the figure is made of bone and sinew, you can still capture emotion through body language and position.

Here is a close up of our mobile monster showing the action captured as the beast rears out of the lava pool. Streaming liquid and other details help add to this effect.

Little details like the crazy laced up motocross boots, as well as the torn pants, all add points of interest.

A bizarre 4x4 truck seemed to fit the bill. The iron-cage wheels filled with molten lava are a neat touch.

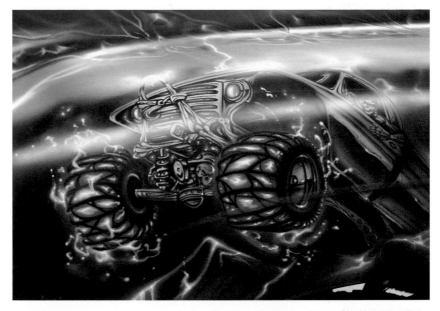

A custom built moto-cross bike doing a tail whip is always cool, especially when the frame is made of bones and the wheels are on fire.

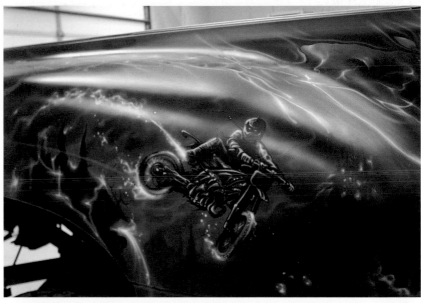

Here is a shot of the tailgate prior to clear coat. Somehow scantily clad ladies appear on the list of things to do in a lot of our commissions.

Speaking of which, I try to show some skin but try not to be too revealing. I guess you could say she's "HOT".

A sort of self portrait, as well as thanks to all the folks involved in the project.

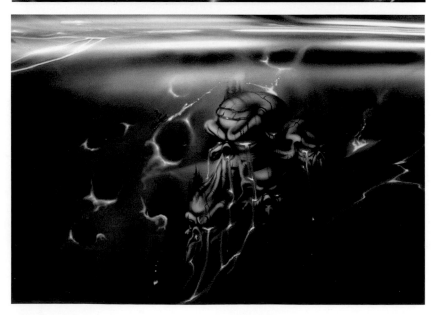

Another part of the painting, a series of mountainous faces, each one dripping with hot lava.

The last thing I do is pinstripe the bumpers so they're not so bald. The rest of the stuff, like the hood and the tonneau cover, are shipped to my shop to be completed there. In fact, the airbrushing of the tonneau cover became the subject of a new Vince Goodeve DVD, now available through our web site or by calling our shop.

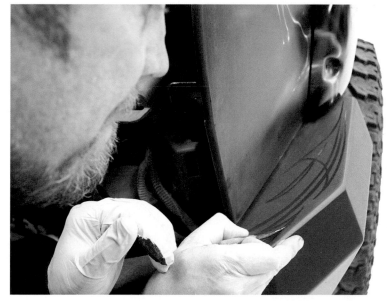

Running the striping brush over the slightly textured bumpers was initially weird, but once I found the groove, a matter of the right speed and consistency, it worked well.

Just a little color or striping in the bumpers ties them into the rest of the truck. We also wanted to give it a moto-cross look that's showing up on some of the super cross bikes

Chapter Thirteen

The Punishment

Using Spontaneous Energy to Create

This project is for my buddy, Dave. His idea of a good time is buying motorcycles and dropping them off at our shop, bellowing as he leaves, "surprise me, and call me when it is done!" Talk about paint-world Nirvana. Since Dave has a distinct taste for the macabre, and isn't really quite right anyway, I came up with the idea of the punishment. I think I ate a bad burrito that day and the misery in my stomach reflected on the mood of the piece. Inspiration is found in the strangest places. The unique thing about this design is, there are no preliminary sketches or reference lines on the tank. I just started airbrushing and this is what happened.

Here's the tank as I shoot from the hip, literally.

Materials List

- Drop dead grey pearl (custom mix)
- PPG's – White, Trans. Maroon, Trans. Purple Trans. Green, Trans Red.
- Tack Rag
- Rich Pen B Series

I paint the tank a custom pearl mix I affectionately call "drop dead grey." A nice starting point upon which to build. After it dries for an hour, I begin developing my shapes and form for the first head. I happily add hooks and various hardware, pulling at the flesh. I always say, "try to paint with the white as if it were going to be your last color."

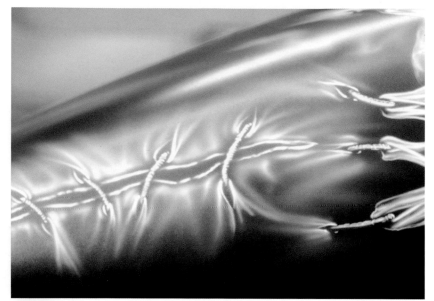

With the face (I use this term lightly) done, I move to the gashes which are sutured or sewn up. Strictly using a nice flowing white, which covers fairly quickly and has little or no tip dry, I build up the light areas of my design. The white mixture is 2 parts medium reducer to 1 part paint or toner. I then add a little slow reducer (just 5 or 6 drops in a gravity feed air brush cup).

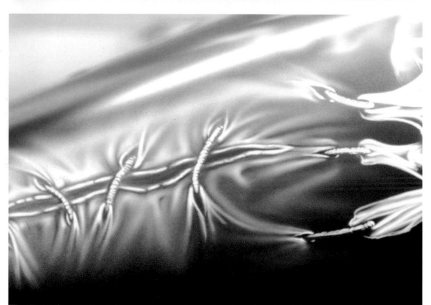

Using transparent maroon only, I work with the shadows I've created with white under-painting, allowing a little overspray to spill over to the contours of my shapes, which gives a nice transition area. Be careful not to obliterate all those textures you rendered in the beginning by blasting too much color over your light areas. The maroon makes a great bridge into the warm grayish base of our main background color.

Using the same technique, I work the features of the tormented face, keeping in mind my light source and with a sense that this is my last step even though it isn't, which forces me to keep tight detail.

When the maroon stage is finished and I'm satisfied with the depth so far, I mist a transparent violet wash on my shadow (or cool) side. In this case it's the right side of the demon. It's subtle, but ads another layer of dimension to the final effect.

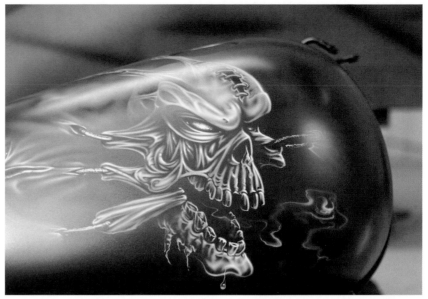

Now adding about 10% to 15% purple to my original trans maroon mixture, I go back in to the shadow areas and push back the darker cracks and caverns or anything that needs to get knocked back another notch. Remember to stay out of your lighter areas and transitions as this color won't jive there.

Next, add a few drops of trans green to your mixture (careful, don't over do it). You should test it on a piece of paper and come up with a very dark color, a kind of black, but of the same color family that you're working with. Use this mixture to enhance the very darkest areas, once again stay out of the light portions, you can't go back to that neighborhood again with these dark colors.

Switching to a trans red color, I intensify the eye and stretched tissues/fibers. I love the interplay of the red against the purple wash we created in the earlier step. It really pushes that side of the face back into space. Next, using white with a few drops of yellow, I hit the highlight edges and give the whole thing the feel of a wet plate of spaghetti.

Just a few more words on freestyle airbrushing. I try not to get too wrapped up in what my final image is going to look like. Relax, let it flow, think of the way the shape of your design grooves with the geometry of the sheet metal. Here, I apply this thinking to the opposite side of the tank.

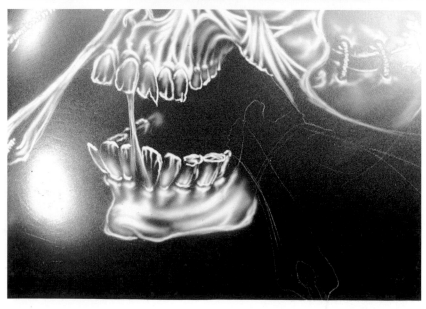

The only rule you should consider is the light source, keep it consistent.

On this side I make the eye a focal point, being sure to pump up the white under-painting and use a circle template to give the iris a crisp edge.

The end result is an image that is solid in the critical areas, but fades nicely into the original background colors, almost giving it an over-exposed look.

The clearcoat only embellishes this effect by marrying all the transparent colors together, and letting the pearls underneath shine through.

Chapter Fourteen

Skulls n' Bones

Everybody Loves a Skull

This project is a simple job, just four pieces for an older Softail. The customer wanted it to be a nice clean black, with simple graphics. The sheet metal came to us in less-than-perfect condition, so the first job was to strip it to bare metal and do all the body work. After applying the primer, we laid a nice coat of black on all the pieces. The owner only wanted art on the tanks, so we put our heads together and decided on a cluster of skulls across each tank, starting large at the front and getting smaller toward the tail end.

Here is a look at our cascading skulls on the left side of the tank during the airbrush stage.

Materials List

- Charcoal filter mask
- Airbrushes: Micron B and Richpen 212 B
- Light Pencil
- Body shop tack rag
- PPG – white
- PPG – Black

After the tank is sandblasted, primed, and prepped (see Prepping the Metal Canvas chapter), I proceed to apply 3 medium wet coats of black basecoat. After allowing it to dry for 8 hours, I'm ready to begin my artwork.

I begin sketching out the basic idea in my head with some white chalk pencil, very loosely and spontaneously. I don't want it to have too much of a contrived look, I want it to look chaotic, like it just happened.

As you see, I've sketched in just the basic lay out, without going into too much detail, because I don't want to be locked in to one design. This way I can freely flow through it without having to worry about catching every line. I'm basically trying to find the balance of the whole thing. I am going to paint some bones sticking out, but I want them to be spontaneous and have not included them in my sketch.

At this point I use an automotive tack rag to wipe off any excess chalk dust. This is important, I don't want to get any of the dust embedded in the job while I'm airbrushing.

The next step is to spray white reduced with medium reducer, 2:1 (two parts reducer and one part paint), then I further reduce it another 5% with slow reducer so that it doesn't spit. I work in the basic shapes in white, keeping in mind my light source and keeping it as tight as possible. Later we will come back in with darker tones to carve out the shadows.

I just keep on rolling with the second skull as I did with the first. I have to be sure to have a good white area where the light hits the skull, so I can come back later and punch out the detail .

Our little bony family grows, all in the same manner, and with the same basic white shapes. Then, I will come back in and elaborate on this later, adding all the nuances and details that are so important.

I slap in the final guy there in the back, and that completes the white faze of the skull area. I've also added a few jagged bones to balance out the design and fill in the negative space around the skulls.

Here I've used a fairly reduced black. I very seldom use black in my artwork, but in this particular job I want the whole thing to be black, white and grey, a very monochromatic looking deal. It's pretty effective. At this point the first skull is done, and I will just work on through the rest, basically finishing them as I go.

Here I've finished the second skull of the line up using the same blackish tones, adding minute details and interesting textures as I progress.

The finished piece. Done in black and white, it jives with all of the accessories and the color scheme of the customer's bike. This is a fairly basic project to pull off. You can charge a very moderate price and still make good money.

Here is the opposite side of the bike. The tank images are similar in balance and composition, but each skull has its own personality. I really try to avoid that stencil-like repetitive look.

I apply 5 or 6 coats of clearcoat to all the parts. After 18 hours of drying, or "gassing off," I wet sand with 2000 grit paper and polish to a mirror-like finish. The fresh black finish and artwork breathe new life into an older bike.

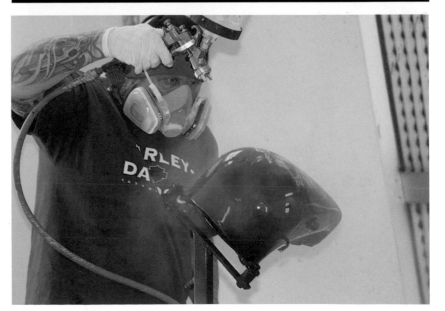

Chapter Fifteen

Crating Your Masterpiece

How to Ship Painted Parts

Now that the painting and polishing are done, and you've had a chance to stand back and admire your work, it's time to box it up and ship it out.

The first step is to find a suitable container. We are fortunate enough to have a Harley-Davidson dealer next door, you may be able to get one of these if you ask, or a little bribery never hurts. So, we start with a steel-bottom motorcycle crate, utilizing the original uprights and cardboard. There are two sizes, both are eight feet long, though one is 29 inches wide, while the other is 48 inches wide. We like to use the biggest one available, it's good to have lots of room, especially if you have lots of small parts to package up.

Inside this seemingly generic cardboard box is a very carefully, meticulously packaged work of art, hidden away from prying eyes and out of harms way until it reaches its final destination.

First order of business is to establish your placement on the crate. We want the frame to be close to the center of the crate, and mounted to the stronger parts of the base. If you have a frame with a tall stretch you will also have to take that into consideration. On this particular project we will be using the mounts for the forward controls to lock the frame into the crate.

On this frame we take the distance between the forward control mounts, and the mount to the crate. We then add about 4 inches to the lower measurement so that the frame is suspended above the crate on the width measurement. We add 3/8 inch to the overall dimension, to allow us to place a small nylon, or plastic (not rubber), washer between the frame and crate.

There are several spots on the frame that are very substantial for attaching points, the motor, foot peg, transmission and swing arm mounts. You don't have to use all of them, every bike is different.

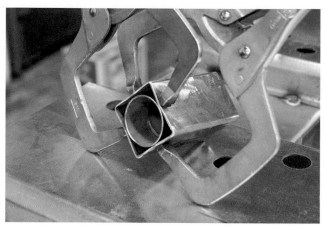

There is no need to use grade A steel to do the job, left over pieces will do just fine when they are properly supported. The square tubing we had was a little thin, so we reinforced it with some round tubing.

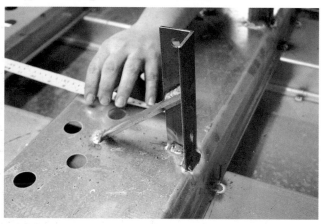

The front mount is the strongest, it must hold the frame from moving front to back, and tilting from side to side. That is why the widest part of the bike is a perfect place to start.

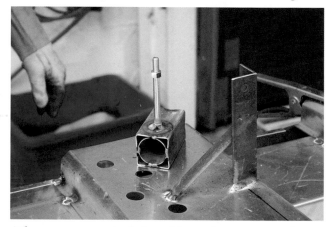

The rear mount is designed in such a manner that we can set the rear of the frame over it without damage, so small is good. You can also see the simple, but effective bracing of the front mount.

This time around we have decided to use the rearmost transmission mount. We must determine the approximate distance from the front position and how tall it should be.

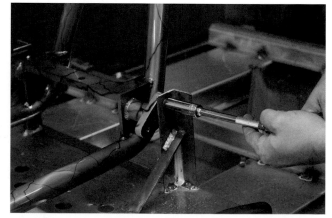

Once the rear mount is built, it is time to fit the frame on the crate. Carefully block up the rear of the frame while you bolt the front in place. Then attach the rear mount prior to welding.

Time to reinstall the frame for the final assembly, so make sure you are happy with your spacing and hardware choices. You want the frame to sit level, so we use long threaded bolts that allow us to raise or lower the frame by using two nuts, one on the bottom and one on the top of the frame to center it. Again, we use nylon or plastic washers so we do not mark the paint.

When the frame is level, and you are happy with the position, you can lock it in place. The reason for not using rubber washers is that the rubber can stain some paint, and it can depress too far and let the bolts come loose. We definitely don't want that to happen.

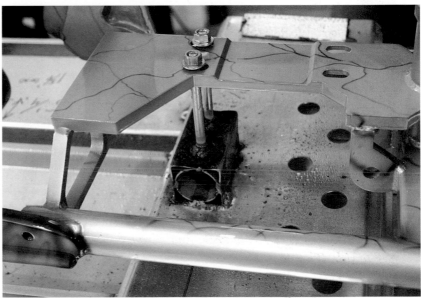

Having everything securely mounted, you can see lots of clearance around the frame. It actually has the appearance of hovering over the crate. Because the front mount does most of the work, the rear one just has to hold it up.

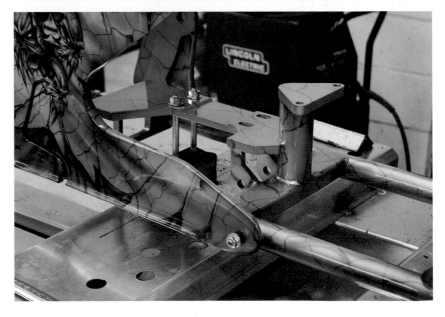

At this point, anything that can be bolted to the frame should be, i.e. the fuel tank, oil tank and so on. The more that can be securely mounted, the less that has to be boxed up. You might have to improvise on mounting if you don't have all of the hardware and/or mounts.

Front fenders usually bolt on the bike using four bolts. We try to design a mount that minimizes contact with the outside of the fender. In this case, we make a mount with two parallel tubes attached to a post

Once we have decided the best location for the mount we weld it in place. If you have time, and enough storage room, it is a good idea to do your welding and mounting on the bike before it is painted. But that wouldn't look very good in a book would it? So we use some shielding so we don't damage the paint.

Once the mount is in place, we bolt up the fender, using plastic or nylon washers. Now the fender is suspended in the middle of nowhere, out of any danger. On big jobs there are always lots of little color matched parts. Fork legs, small mounts and all the rest. Any small parts can now be carefully wrapped and boxed up (note image below). Using straps, securely mount the box at the rear of the skid, out of the way.

Now is the time to do your final inspection and make sure all of the parts are there. The crate can be covered, using uprights and cardboard, or plywood and 2x4s. We will use the original steel uprights and cardboard. If the bike is being shipped out of the country make sure to leave a window so that customs can look in without removing the cover. A special thanks to Dan Metzger for his input and helping us crate up paint jobs for the last 4 years.

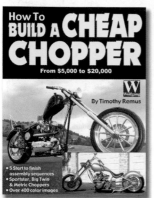

HOW TO BUILD A CHEAP CHOPPER

Choppers don't have to cost $30,000.00. In fact, a chopper built at home can be had for as little as $5,000.00. Watch the construction of 4 inexpensive choppers with complete start-to-finish photo sequences. Least expensive are metric choppers, based on a 1970s vintage Japanese four-cylinder drivetrain installed in an hardtail frame. Next up are three bikes built using Buell/Sportster drivetrains. The fact is, a complete used Buell or Sportster is an inexpensive motorcycle – and comes with wheels and tires, transmission, brakes and all the rest. Just add a hardtail frame and accessories to suit. Most expensive is bike number 4. This big-twin chopper uses a RevTech drivetrain set in a Rolling Thunder frame. Written by Tim Remus. Shot in the shops of Brian Klock, Motorcycle Works, Redneck Engineering and Dave Perewitz this book uses numerous photos to Illustrate the construction of these 4 bikes.

Eleven Chapters   144 Pages $24.95   Over 400 photos-100% color

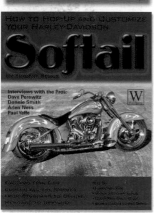

HOW TO BUILD A SOFTAIL

Got a Softail? Got a hankering to separate yours from all the other Softails parked outside the bar? Search no farther than this new book, How To Hop-Up and Customize Your Harley-Davidson Softail, from well-known author Timothy Remus. Whether your goal is to personalize that two-wheeled ride or give it more than 60 horsepower, the ideas and answers you need are right here.

Learn how to install a 95 inch kit with over 100 horsepower, add a 250 rear tire, lower the bike, and add extended fuel tanks. Make yours faster, sexier and more personal with this all-color book from Timothy Remus and Wolfgang Publications.

How to: Lower Your Bike
            Design a Custom Softail
            Install New Sheet Metal
            Build a Budget 95 Inch Motor

Nine Chapters   144 Pages $24.95   Over 300 photos-100% color

HOP-UP & CUSTOMIZE YOUR H-D BAGGER

Baggers don't have to be slow, and they don't have to look like every other Dresser in the parking lot. Take your Bagger from slow to show with a few more cubic inches, a little paint and some well placed accessories. Whether you're looking for additional power or more visual pizazz, the answers and ideas you need are contained in this new book from Tim Remus.

Follow the project bike from start to finish, including a complete dyno test and remapping of the fuel injections. Includes two 95 inch engine make overs.
How to:
• Pick the best accessories for the best value
• Install a lowering kit
• Do custom paint on a budget
• Create a unique design for your bike

Eight Chapters   144 Pages $24.95   Over 400 full-color photos

ADVANCED AIRBRUSH ART

Like a video done with still photography, this new book is made up entirely of photo sequences that illustrate each small step in the creation of an airbrushed masterpiece. Watch as well-known masters like Vince Goodeve, Chris Cruz, Steve Wizard and Nick Pastura start with a sketch and end with a NASCAR helmet or motorcycle tank covered with graphics, murals, pinups or all of the above.

Interviews explain each artist's preference for paint and equipment, and secrets learned over decades of painting. Projects include a chrome eagle surrounded by reality flames, a series of murals, and a variety of graphic designs.
This is a great book for anyone who takes their airbrushing seriously and wants to learn more.

Ten Chapters   144 Pages $24.95   Over 400 photos, 100% color

ADVANCED CUSTOM PAINTING TECHNIQUES

When it comes to custom painting, there is one name better known than all the others, and that name is Jon Kosmoski. Whether the project in your shop rides on two wheels or four, whether you're trying to do a simple kandy job or complex graphics, this how-to book from Jon Kosmoski is sure to answer your questions. Chapters one through three cover Shop Equipment, Gun Control and Paint Materials. Chapters four through seven get to the heart of the matter with complete start-to-finish painting sequences.

- Shop set up
- Gun Control
- Use of new paint materials
- 4 start-to-finish sequences
- Two wheels or four
- Simple or complex
- Kandy & Klear

Seven Chapters   144 Pages $24.95   Over 350 photos, 100% color

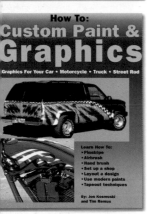

HOW TO: CUSTOM PAINT & GRAPHICS

A joint effort of the master of custom painting, Jon Kosmoski and Tim Remus, this is the book for anyone who wants to try their hand at dressing up their street rod, truck or motorcycle with lettering, flames or exotic graphics.

7 chapters include:
- Shop tools and equipment
- Paint and matcrials
- Letter & pinstripe by hand
- Design and tapeouts
- Airbrushing
- Hands-on, Flames and signs
- Hands-on, Graphics

Seven Chapters   144 Pages $24.95   Over 250 photos, 50% in color

ULTIMATE SHEET METAL FABRICATION

In an age when most products are made by the thousands, many yearn for the one-of-kind metal creation. Whether you're building or restoring a car, motorcycle, airplane or (you get the idea), you'll find the information you need to custom build your own parts from steel or aluminum.

11 chapters include:
- Layout a project
- Pick the right material
- Shrinkers & stretchers
- English wheel
- Make & use simple tooling
- Weld aluminum or steel
- Use hand and power tools

Eleven Chapters   144 Pages $19.95   Over 350 photos

ADVANCED SHEET METAL FABRICATION

Advanced Sheet Metal Fabrication Techniques, is a photo-intensive how-to book. See Craig Naff build a Rolls Royce fender, Rob Roehl create a motorcycle gas tank, Ron Covell form part of a quarter midget body and Fay Butler shape an aircraft wheel fairing. Methods and tools include English wheel, power hammer, shrinkers and stretchers, and of course the hammer and dolly.

- Sequences in aluminum and steel
- Multi-piece projects
- Start to finish sequences
- From building the buck to shaping the steel
- Includes interviews with the metal shapers
- Automotive, motorcycle and aircraft

7 Chapters   144 Pages $24.95   144 pages, over 300 photos - 60% color

Sources

Andrew Mack & Son Brush Co.
225 East Chicago St., PO Box 157
Jonesville, Michigan 49250
(517) 849- 9272
Mackbrush.com

Art Essentials of New York Inc.
P.O Box 38, Tallman, NY 10982-0038
(800) 283-5323
Artessentialsofnewyork.com

Art Video Productions
PO Box 92343
Pasadena, CA 91109
(877) 227-8843 in the USA
(770) 206-7478 outside the USA
Artvideostore.com

Bear Air Express
20 Hampden Drive #2
S. Easton, MA 02375
(800) BearAir
Bearair.com

Coates & Best Inc.
883 2nd Avenue East
Owen Sound, ON N4K 2H2
(519) 376-5499

Blick Art Materials
P.O. Box 1267
Galesburg, IL 61402-1267
(800) 828-4548
(309) 343-6181 (International)
Dickblick.com

Fox Harley-Davidson
Hwy 6/10 @ Story Book Park Road
P.O. Box 817 Owen Sound
Ontario, Canada
N4K 5W9
(519) 371-6666
foxharleydavidson.com

Houseofkolor.com
Distributor: D&E Distributors
2709 – 44th Avenue
Vernon, BC V1T 8E9
(250) 542-6788

Notablesigns
3112 Braley Road
Ransomville, NY 14131
(716) 751-3708
notablesigns@aol.com

PPG World Headquarters
One PPG Place
Pittsburgh, PA 15272
(412) 434-3131
PPG.com

Scenic City Automotive
1010 9th Avenue West
Owen Sound, ON N4K 5R7
(519) 376-7310

Sign Gold Corporation
53 Smith Road
Middletown, NY 10941
(845) 692-6565
Signgold.com

WJT Graphic supplies
WJT Distributing Inc.
160 Bentley St.
Markham, Ontario
L3R-3L2, Canada
(800) 465-8650